THREE SMALLER WISDOM BOOKS

Lao Zi's *Dao De Jing*,
The Great Learning (Da Xue), and the
Doctrine of the Mean (Zhong Yong)

Translated with Introductions
and Commentaries by
Patrick Edwin Moran

UNIVERSITY
PRESS OF
AMERICA

Lanham • New York • London

Copyright © 1993 by
University Press of America®, Inc.
4720 Boston Way
Lanham, Maryland 20706

3 Henrietta Street
London WC2E 8LU England

Library of Congress Cataloging-in-Publication Data

Moran, Patrick Edwin.
Three smaller wisdom books : Lao Zi's Dao de jing, the
Great learning (Da xue), and the Doctrine of the mean
(Zhong yong) / translated with introductions and
commentaries by Patrick Edwin Moran.
p.   cm.
Includes bibliographical references and index.
1. Lao-tzu. Tao te ching.   2. Ta hsüeh.   3. Chung yung.
I. Lao-tzu. Tao te ching. English. 1993.   II. Ta hsüeh. English,
1993.   III. Chung yung. English. 1993.   IV. Title.
Bl1900.L35M66   1993   181'.11—dc20   93–25236 CIP

ISBN 0–8191–9214–7 (cloth : alk. paper)
ISBN 0–8191–9251–5 (pbk. : alk. paper)

The paper used in this publication meets the minimum requirements of
American National Standard for Information Sciences—Permanence
of Paper for Printed Library Materials, ANSI Z39.48–1984.

For
Mamie N. Gaskill
Carol Gunlach
Lillian Hanks
Sara Jane Whitten
Doris McGaffey

Unobtrusive farers on the Way

Acknowledgements

Nobody writes translations in a vacuum. I was introduced to Chinese philosophy through Arthur Waley's beautiful *Three Ways of Thought in Ancient China*. Over the years I have read every translation of the *Lao Zi* that I could find, including Arthur Waley's *The Way and Its Power*. Of these many translations, those of D. C. Lau and Wing-tsit Chan have been constantly at my side in teaching and living. I have frequently used both of those translations in my own courses over the past couple of decades. In going back to compare my translation with the translations of others, I find that mine is most like Chan's. Part of the reason is that we both prefer to stay close to the sentence structure of the original, but it is also probably true that Chan's words have gradually permeated my subconscious. Of all of the translations that I have used, I still find his the best. He wrote, however, without the benefit of the two texts written on silk that lay entombed for more than two thousand years at Ma-Wang Dui in China. Those texts, unearthed in 1973, form the basis for another outstanding translation of the *Lao Zi,* that of Robert G. Henricks. I am grateful for the work of these earlier translators, and for the translations of all of the others mentioned in the bibliography.

I am very thankful for the efforts of my teacher, Aisin-gioro Yu-yun, who guided my early study of the *Great Learning* and the *Doctrine of the Mean* and helped me form my interpretation of the idea of integrity (*cheng* 誠) that makes one of the main connections between those two texts.

I also owe a great debt of thanks to another teacher, Yan Ling-feng, professor of philosophy at National Taiwan University and an eminent expert on the *Lao Zi*, who most graciously went over the entire text, line by line, with me. While my interpretations differ substantially from theirs at points, the translations would be much poorer had I been deprived of the help of these two scholars, each of whom is in his own way dedicated to the Way that these works attempt to convey.

I would also like to express gratitude to all of my students. Special thanks go to Michael Sierra, who entered the entire Chinese text of the *Lao Zi* out of his own enthusiasm for the book; Jonathan Zuber, who removed many of the errors of spelling and grammar from my translations and notes; and Christian Hall, who helped proofread the Chinese texts of the *Great Learning* and *Doctrine of the Mean.*

Dana Hutchens, of Wake Forest University Public Affairs, and Mame Verdinek, the secretary for East Asian Languages and Literatures, have scrutinized the entire book, looking for (and finding) errors of all kinds. Mame Verdinek has also helped with the electronic typesetting procedures as well as helping to keep me on the track during the time when I was finishing these translations.

I should also like to thank the institutions, Grinnell College and Wake Forest University, that have provided the environment for study under which these translations were written.

I have used the section titles from the edition of the *Da Xue* (*Great Learning*) published by the San-min Shu-ju.

Table of Contents

Preface

We set a high standard of moral excellence for people in our culture, but judging by the results, we do not know very much about how to secure the actualization of the ideals we propound. We set before our young people the demand that each of them should become a certain kind of human being. We specify the end result that we want. However, we give them no clear path toward that goal. Sometimes they succeed, possibly because of the presence of good role models; more often, they muddle through somehow, and far too often they fail. When they fail, we speak of them as bad people and seek to wreak vengeance upon them. While that course of action may bring its own satisfactions to some, it has not proven effective in preventing further problems. All of us suffer because of the difficulties troubling those who do not succeed in the life of the spirit.

One of the main strengths of Chinese society has been that it has a methodology for producing people who are at peace both with themselves and with the other members of society. The tools of the Chinese social environment can indeed be misused by both the family and the larger society to take unfair advantage of the individual, but that should not obscure the positive features that are displayed when the society lives up to its highest potentials. Chinese society has at times indeed been turned into a bedlam of hatred, reprisal, and search for various kinds of personal aggrandizement, most recently and prominently in the so-called "Great Cultural Revolution." Even during such times, people of immensely strong moral fibre, people who are loving and responsible to their friends and neighbors, have nevertheless been produced.

An awareness that these three books of ancient Chinese wisdom had some of the answers concerning how our own society might better pursue its goals recommended their study to me decades ago. To the general reader I now present, in as clear a form as I know how, the insights and wisdom preserved in them. I regret that I will surely be found to have fallen short in some respects, and request that my readers give me their criticisms.

I have chosen to use the modern *pin-yin* romanization and have prepared some hints on pronunciation (which appear after the translations) to help the reader who may be unfamiliar with this system of notation. In addition, I have chosen to regard the word *dao* 道 (way) as an English word, and from this point on I will not italicize it. In keeping with my decision to use the *pin-yin* romanization system, I have also changed the spelling of "Taoist" to "Daoist." Those changes may make it a little easier for the student new to this field to remember that "dao" is pronounced like the first syllable of the word dowager, and not like Taos, New Mexico.

Symbols Used

⟨ ⟩   delete the enclosed text

[ ]   insert the enclosed text

( )   use the enclosed text as an explanation

{ }   tentative emendation

INTRODUCTION
TO
THE
LAO ZI

General Remarks

To a world that believes more and more in the efficacy of coercion, the *Lao Zi* poses an alternative. To a species that is driving itself and its ecosystem to extinction, the *Lao Zi* gives a warning. To the parent or teacher who feels forced to use coercion, the *Lao Zi* offers kindly advice. To the individual human being who finds him- or herself staggering under guilt inculcated by parents or other authority figures, the *Lao Zi* offers a possible way out.

This great book, which is small in number of words, has received much attention lately. I originally made this translation for my students so that they could have a record at hand of what I think the text means while at the same time they might study other translations or study the original Chinese. Now I hope that it may serve as a basis for study by others.

As I will explain in greater detail below, my translation is based on a revised text that brings together the efforts of generations upon generations of scholars who have tried to make a full recovery of a supreme work of art that must originally have been carried down, falteringly, in an oral tradition. My revised text combines the recensions available before this century with the two texts written on silk that were recovered in 1973 from the tombs at Ma-Wang Dui 馬王堆 (usually called in Chinese the *Bo-shu Lao Zi* 帛書老子). I have given the Chinese text in the recension of Wang Bi 王弼 (226–249), the version that is generally regarded as the best of the traditional texts, and have added to that text (and noted) such emendations as seem to me correct.

If the reader has not previously examined other interpretations of the text, it would be my hope that at some time he or she would compare my translation with those of others. The *Lao Zi* is difficult to translate because the subject matter is often far from the experiences of the everyday world, and because the author or authors most often omit the subjects of sentences. So sometimes it is difficult to know, for instance, whether a sentence is meant to apply to the Way (*Dao* 道), or whether it is meant to apply to the Sage (*sheng ren* 聖人) who follows that Dao. Of course there are occasionally more serious difficulties.

In general, I would prefer to let the text speak for itself. But part of the joy and the challenge of reading this text is that after a thorough immersion in it the general approach of its author or authors begins to shine through and to illuminate passages that on the first reading seemed not to have major import. Therefore I have occasionally ventured to add my own commentaries to the chapters in the hope that I may alert the reader to more possibilities of interpretation. Of course, the reader will also benefit on this score from studying alternative translations.

Victor H. Mair, *Tao Te Ching,* has reached much the same conclusions on the authorship and oral nature of the text as have I. His translation is well worth study.

The Question of Authorship

Tradition claims that the author of this book was an older contemporary of Confucius (551 – 479). The language of the text, however, does not even retain the ancient elements still to be seen in the writings of Zhuang Zi 莊子 (Chuang Tzu, c. 369 – c. 286), much less display the archaic nature of the *Analects of Confucius* and earlier books. Most modern authorities date the text at around the end of the Zhou dynasty, or approximately 250 B.C.

The word *zi* 子 that forms the second element of "Lao Zi" simply means Master, and is the normal term of respect given to Chinese philosophers. For instance, Confucius is the Latinized form of Kong Fu Zi 孔夫子, or Grand Master Kong. Mencius is the Latinized form of Meng Zi 孟子, or Master Meng. Kong and Meng being Chinese surnames, we might reasonably expect that Lao老 would be another surname, but it is not. Lao in this case is simply the Chinese word that means old. So Lao Zi probably means old master, or old teacher. But Chinese does not distinguish between singular and plural nouns. So Lao Zi may also mean the old masters. Who might this old master or these old masters be?

Chinese nouns do not give any indication of gender, so we do not have any reason to attribute a definite sexual identity to that this old teacher or these old masters.

We are left to appreciate a philosophy that cannot be pegged to any definite time or author. As I shall attempt to show below, even though the text appears not to have been written down before the closing years of the Zhou dynasty, the **words** may have been transmitted in an oral tradition from a time even earlier than that of Confucius.

For the sake of convenience I shall speak as though this book was authored by one man whose name was Lao Zi. The reader should note that the biographical information about the author in early histories such as the *Shi Ji* 史記 *(Records of the Grand Historian of China)* of Si-ma Qian 司馬遷 (died 110 B.C.) has more the character of legend than of true history.

Some Opinions about the Text

My translation differs from those of others for several reasons. After studying the silk texts I have changed my mind about the advisability of "tampering" with the received text. I have decided that the process of trying to figure out what the intended text and meaning may be has been one in which scholars have been engaged since almost the very beginning. There may never have been a "correct" written version. Any time new information comes into the scholarly community, it is possible to make improvements on the text. So my translation reflects what, after careful consideration, I believe to be what the original author or authors intended to say.

Recently, some scholars have given indications that they believe the silk texts to be better than the received text. However, if we had the silk texts but did not have the received text to guide our understanding of them, I think we would frequently find them impossible to understand.

If we look at the silk versions, and even use one to complement the other, we see that they form a rather poor text. There are several kinds of problems with it. I will list the main difficulties below, and return to give many specific illustrations later, in the body of the translation.

There are very, very many cases where only what is properly the phonetic component for the intended world was written. For instance, *wei* 謂, which means to speak of as, is a combination of the character *yan* 言, which indicates that the character has something to do with speech, and *wei* 胃, which means stomach but is used here as an indication of pronunciation. However, in the silk versions, stomach is frequently written for to speak of as. Since the modern pronunciation of these two characters is the same, and since *wei* 胃 appears frequently in the text, that particular character would be easy to guess. Nevertheless, there are many such defective characters, and not all of them would yield so easily to analysis.

There are also many cases where a substitution of radicals is made, as when *qing* 請 (please) is written for *jing* 精 (refined). Again, if the surrounding text is not too corrupt, then these substitutions are easy to figure out.

Also, the silk texts may add a radical to what appears in the received text, as when the silk texts write *wang* 忘 (forget) for *wang* 亡 (perish). In this particular instance there is real question about the meaning intended by the author.

In a few cases, the scribes who copied the silk texts write synonyms, as when *wu* 沕 (hidden in the depths) is written for *mo* 沒 (to sink).

Sometimes cognates are written for the character in the received text, as when *ming* 命 (to name, to command, ancient pronunciation *miang*) is written for *ming* 名 (name, ancient pronunciation *mieng*).

In some cases homonyms are substituted for what must be the correct character, as when *xing* 省 (inspect) is written for *xing* 姓 (surname). In other cases, near homonyms are used, as when *zhi* 志 (aspirations, ancient pronunciation *tiêg*) is written for *shi* 識 (recognition, ancient pronunciation *siêg*). Some substitutions of this sort could cause the unprepared reader much doubt and confusion.

Occasionally the silk texts substitute words with similar meanings and similar pronunciations for what is in the received text, as when *fu* 頁 (ancient pronunciation *b'iug*, meaning to lean on) is written for *bei* 倍 (ancient pronunciation *b'wêg*, meaning to support). Subtle differences of meaning of this kind could be very perplexing without the guidance of the received text.

Another kind of problem with the silk texts is that sometimes a word is used phonetically, but it does not happen to be the phonetic component for the character that is now found at that place in the text. For instance, *xi* 昔 (bygone times) is written for *zuo* 作 (to make, to rise up), and *rui* 芮 (minuscule) is written for *tui* 退 (to recede, turn back). In the first case we may venture the guess that the scribe is still trying to write *zuo* since Bernard Karlgren (*Grammata Serica Recensa*) gives the ancient pronunciation of the former as *siak* (and gives the ancient pronunciation of a related character, *cuo* 厝, as *ts'ak*) — which is very close to the ancient pronunciation of *zuo*, which is *ts'ak*. But in the second case, the first character has the ancient pronunciation *niwad* whereas the second character has the ancient pronunciation *t'wâd*, so it seems rather less likely that the scribe was trying to write an equivalent of the modern character. In any event, the intended meanings would be hard to discover if we had only the silk texts.

I will have more to say about the textual problems later; the question I want the reader to consider now is this: Under what circumstances would a literate, intelligent, and indeed a careful scribe with good calligraphy spend countless hours writing out a text with so many obvious mistakes and variations that cannot be accounted for as simple copying errors (as when *ben* 本 becomes separated into two parts and appears as *da shi* 大十)?

Much has been said about how the silk texts are better than the received texts such as the Wang Bi version because they frequently give clear guidelines for the intended structure of a sentence. They include characters whose function is to indicate grammatical relationships. At the very least, they tell us how the scribe who wrote that particular version of the text thought the sentence ought to be understood.

If these characters indicating grammatical relationships were originally present in the text, then why would later scribes systematically remove them?

I think the most likely answer is that neither of the silk texts was the direct ancestor of the texts we have today. It makes no sense to me to assume that some scribe deleted useful grammatical information from the text while at the same time succeeding in fixing most of the incorrect characters. I suppose it is barely possible that one person effaced the grammatical and structural indicators and later on another person took that text as the basis for his attempt to correct the characters. But I think there is a more reasonable and instructive hypothesis.

Let us reconsider some of the above observations: The silk texts were written with characters that frequently conserved only the phonetic information that the scribe was attempting to convey. At other times words were written with characters having different radicals, or were replaced by synonyms, homonyms, or cognates. (Of course, much of the time the characters were entirely correct by present-day standards.)

When do people make such mistakes and changes? I think the most obvious case would be when various people were independently trying to write down a text that had been passed to them through an oral tradition. They knew how to recite the piece of literature. Its meaning had been explained to them. But they were not necessarily sure of how to write it out. They probably did not have a dictionary at hand. They were most concerned to get this precious cultural artifact down on paper. Sometimes they remembered the sounds, but couldn't think of how they ought to be written. They might, in such a case, write a homonym. Sometimes they not only wrote something intended as the phonetic component for a character, but also added an element intended to give a finer indication of the meaning. However, one or both elements may not have been what was then or what later became accepted for the written form of that word. Sometimes they could not remember the sound, but they remembered the meaning of the passage, so they wrote a synonym. And, of course, much of the time they succeeded in writing the correct characters. Two such early texts, which appear to have a family resemblance, are the A and B silk texts discovered at Ma-Wang Dui.

Now consider that this process of transcription most likely happened many times. If the *Lao Zi* existed for some time in the oral tradition, or even if it were once written down, later destroyed, and still later reconstituted from the minds of those who had memorized it, then there would almost certainly have been several written versions. Doubtless there were substantial variations in their quality.

The several versions that I hypothesize to have existed must have been compared, and a fairly consistent and accepted text prepared by around the end of the Zhou dynasty, because small segments of the *Lao Zi* are quoted in various early philosophical texts, and in them there are only minor variations from the received texts.

The Wang Bi text is itself imperfect, and in one instance it has the kind of error most common to the silk texts — it has only the phonetic component of a character and omits the part intended to clarify its meaning. In chapter eight, the Wang Bi text has *zheng* 正 (upright) where context and a very large number of other texts indicate the meaning should be *zheng* 政 (to make people be upright, i.e., to govern). It is possible that the text was originally correct and someone made an error in copying, but it is also possible that it was carried down through the tradition to Wang Bi's hand in the incorrect form and Wang failed to correct it.

Other errors in the Wang Bi text are more interesting because they show the utility of the silk texts. I will discuss some of them below.

It is frequently argued that the sequence of the *Lao Zi* has been disordered because the text was physically randomized. It was, scholars say, originally written on long slips of bamboo called *jian* 簡 that were joined together with cord in much the same way that a lath snow fence or a bamboo window curtain is made. Later on the cords rotted away in storage, thus forcing someone to try to put all of the bamboo slips back in proper sequence. When that person occasionally failed to restore the proper sequence, error was introduced.

The hidden assumption behind the shuffled sequence (*cuo jian* 錯簡) theory is that sensible phrases were confined to single slips of bamboo. Of course the truth was that most phrases were split among two or more bamboo slips, and that only the occasional phrase could be shifted without spoiling the proper sequence of words in sentences. So it is most likely that if a number of errors exist due to shuffled sequence, then they must have been made by shuffling the bamboo slips in many successive generations of text, and the arrangement of text on the bamboo slips had to have been different in different generations. But there is another possible explanation for the kinds of errors that appear in the text.

Not only is it difficult to account for very many transpositions by assuming most of them were caused by shuffling the sequence of bamboo slips, but that scenario also does not account for the frequent duplication of passages found in the *Lao Zi*. Scholars have argued that those repetitions were not intentional. It would have been rare for one sensible phrase to have been isolated on one slip of bamboo and so be undetected when moved to a different chapter, but it would have been impossible for the same slip of bamboo to duplicate itself and appear several times in the same book. Yet that is what we seem to see, and it is difficult to explain how these duplications might have occurred on the assumption that we are dealing with a written text. However, if the original units were memorized phrases or verses instead of strips of bamboo, then it is easy to understand how lapses of recall and trains of association could account both for phrases or blocks of phrases cropping up in odd places and even for their getting duplicated from time to time.

Why would the *Lao Zi* have been passed down through a fallible oral tradition? The early Daoists may have frowned upon writing. Moreover, Daoists were dissident thinkers. They clearly did not favor the prevailing Confucian values of their time, and it is possible that the authorities did not like those people There may have been a time when it would have been dangerous to write out the text of the *Lao Zi*. Memorization of the *Lao Zi* would not only have been more secure, but would also have performed the functions of indoctrination and maintenance of group solidarity. We need not assume that the early Daoists set out to achieve those two results to observe that keeping the *Lao Zi* in the oral tradition would have had survival value for the Daoist movement, however that movement may have been constituted. Also, it is well known that written versions of other texts were destroyed and the texts later recovered from the memories of the scholars who could recite them.

Cases where Information in the Silk Texts Helps Correct or Interpret the Traditional Text

In chapter twenty-one, one character has two possible interpretations, and an alternate character in the silk texts helps determine which meaning to choose. The traditional text has the word *yue* 閱, which may mean either to dispense (as provisions are dispensed from a granary) or to inspect. The silk texts have *shun* 順, which means to flow along with. It is possible to interpret the text in terms of this other meaning, as do D. C. Lau and Robert G. Henricks. However, observation of the other chapters in the silk text shows that they frequently write homonyms for the correct character. According to the ancient pronunciations deduced by Bernard Karlgren, *shun* 順 and *xun* 巡 were close in pronunciation in ancient times (as they are today), and share their phonetic component. *Xun* means to make an inspection tour. So I conclude that the intended meaning was to inspect, and that various scribes represented this meaning by writing different characters.

In chapter twenty-six, the traditional text has the correct meaning, but an incorrect character that does not properly rhyme. The traditional text has *ben* 本 (root) and some other versions have *chen* 臣 (official). The word *chen* seems to be preferred because it preserves the rhyme scheme of the chapter, but its meaning is difficult to interpret in that context. The silk texts, however, write *gen* 根 (root), which preserves the meaning given in the traditional text and also restores the proper rhyme. In this case, the silk texts reassure us of the correctness of the meaning given in the Wang Bi version (The same variant is seen in other early texts.)

In chapter twenty-seven, the traditional text has a character that can be interpreted according to its face meaning, but may be interpreted according to the meaning of a homonym. The ancient pronunciations of *xi* 襲 (to enshroud, to double, to follow, to repeat, to imitate) and *xi* 習 (to practice) are almost the same. As D. C. Lau points out on page 306 of his recent translation, the B silk text has *yi* 曳 which is probably intended to be *yi* 愧 (the same character with the heart radical added at the left). That character means to practice, and so supports those commentaries that interpret *xi* 襲 to mean *xi* 習.

In chapter twenty-nine, one phrase has four alternative characters among the traditional texts, a fifth from the A silk text, and a sixth from the B silk text. The phrase follows in series with several others that involve opposites, but the words used in this phrase in the Wang Bi version are not opposites. By assuming one particular character to be the correct original one we can account for the presence of all the other characters not found in the Wang Bi version, and may account for Wang Bi's character. By this interpretation, *pei* 培 was the originally intended and correct character. It changed into *jie* 接 because of the similarity of their forms. *Jie* may next have turned into *cuo* 挫, the character found in Wang Bi's version, because of similarity of both form and of ancient pronunciation. *Pei* 培 turned into *zai* 載 presumably because someone remembered one meaning of *pei* and tried to note that meaning down by writing *zai*. (See Zhu Qing-yuan, *Lao Zi Jiao-shi*, p. 75.) *Pei* 培 turned into *pei* 陪 by the substitution of an incorrect radical. *Pei* 培 turned into *pei* 坏 because the ancient forms of their phonetic components are very similar. (See the *Shuo Wen Jie Zi* or the *Zhong Wen Da Ci Dian*.)

In chapter sixty-two, the silk texts have a fully-formed character, *he* 賀 (to congratulate) where the received texts have only a phonetic, *jia* 加 (to add). The explanations given by commentators on the traditional text, and the translations I have seen of that passage, all seem forced to me. Nevertheless, D. C. Lau corrects the silk texts to conform to the Wang Bi text. I accept the silk text version because it does not require a forced interpretation, and because it is easy to see how the error might' have occurred in the other texts.

In chapter seventy-six where the destruction of a tree is mentioned, the Wang Bi text has a character (*bing* 兵, weapon —> edged tool) that gives approximately the correct meaning, although its usage is odd. One other received text gives a character whose meaning seems to fit the passage (*zhe* 折, to break). Other received texts offer several alternatives (*gong* 共, *gong* 拱, *gong* 栱), all of which are similar in pronunciation to each other, but substantially different from the first two characters mentioned. The meanings of the latter group of characters all seem inappropriate to the context. The fact that their meanings are wrong while their sounds are similar suggests that various scribes were writing a word phonetically. The A silk text, however, uses a character whose pronunciation is similar to theirs (*heng* 恆). This instance appears to be another in which a phonetic component is written for an entire character. And that character (*geng* 椢) is even closer in its modern pronunciation to the earlier group of characters. *Geng* 椢 means for a tree to reach its natural limit of life. It is related to the character *geng* 亙 that means the extreme limit of something. Furthermore, it is related to another character (*geng* 埂) that means the pathway leading up to a grave. The B silk text gives *jing* 兢, which means respectful, fear, caution, and which some say is a mistake for *jing* 競 meaning to compete but with an ancient pronunciation similar to the other characters in the series mentioned above. D. C. Lau has given us the key for this character (see his *Lao Zi: Tao Te Ching*, p. 256).

It is interesting that most of the places where the silk texts make possible major improvements in the traditional text are located from chapter twenty-one to chapter twenty-nine. It may be that the Wang Bi text derives from a line of texts that was damaged in some way throughout that range.

Passages that Remain Difficult to Translate

It seems to me that chapter thirteen must have something seriously wrong with it. Some authorities try to translate the text as it stands, but their translations all seem forced. The alternative is to make fairly major changes in the text. Unfortunately, the silk texts do not help much in this endeavor. Even after attempting to improve the text, it is still difficult to interpret. I have changed the text as radically as I dare, but still do not feel that the exact intent of the author can be confidently stated. Readers of this translation are urged to compare my attempt with the translations of others.

Chapter sixty is another text that is difficult to interpret. I remain dissatisfied both with the theoretical explanations offered for this chapter, and with explanations of its grammatical structure.

Recommendations to the Student

There are many good translations available. Each one represents the understanding of the text reached by an individual. Such an understanding is based in part on that individual's reading of explanations by others concerning what the text means, and in part on that person's own life experience.

The most meaningful understanding of the text will be the one that you form for yourself by trying to relate what you read to your own life. Comparing different translations may cast a different light on what Lao Zi has to say to you. I am personally convinced that while parts of the text are crystal clear, nobody knows what the author means in every case. So you might as well have your own interpretation and your own sense of just how shaky that interpretation may be.

TRANSLATION
OF
THE
LAO ZI

第一章

道：可道（導），非常道；
名：可名，非常名。
無名，天地之始。
有名，萬物之母。
故
常無欲，以觀其妙；
常有欲，以觀其徼。
此兩者，同出而異名。
同謂之玄。
玄之又玄，眾妙之門。

1.

A way (dao) that one can be directed along[1] is not the constant Dao.
A name that can be given is not a constant name.
Nameless is the beginning of Heaven and Earth.
Named is the mother of the myriad creatures.
So,
It is always by desirelessness that one sees the hidden (noumenal) aspect,[2]
And always by being in a state of having desires that one observes the outer (phenomenal) aspect.[3]
These two [aspects of all reality] emerge together and are differently named.
Together, they are called the dark and mysterious.[4]
The most dark and mysterious of the dark and mysterious
Is the portal of the multitudinous wonders.[5]

NOTES:

1. This meaning of dao 道 was already present in the *Analects of Confucius*. Confucius lived from 551 to 479 B.C. The common translation "to speak about" is a derivative meaning of narrower scope that did not achieve currency until it appeared in the *Xun Zi* 荀子 and the related texts in the *Li Ji* 禮記 *(Book of Rites)*. Xun Zi lived from about 298 to 238 B.C. Many people believe that the *Lao Zi* was not written down before the final years of the Zhou dynasty, which ended in 221 B.C., but it may have been carried down from a much earlier time in the oral tradition. In any event, the earlier meaning of dao is correct and adequate in this context.

2. *Miao,* inexplicable efficacies.

3. *Jiao*, outer fringes of things.

4. *Xuan,* far, obscure, deep, profound, abstruse, subtle.

5. *Miao,* inexplicable efficacies.

Commentary:

See the first appendix for two alternative interpretations of this chapter, and for the explanation of its deep structure. In that appendix I show alternate punctuations for chapter one, and give a more complete philosophical and philological analysis.

Note that Chapter 34 uses the expression "without desire" much as it is used here.

In general, the Daoists regard desire as a source of subjective bias. We all know from personal experience that we lose objectivity when our desires are allowed to gain sway. But this first chapter of the *Lao Zi* indicates that desirelessness is not to be absolutely preferred over desirefulness. Rather, they are two modalities by which our world may be perceived. When one achieves a state of desirelessness, one can have mystic unity with the entire universe. But the outer, phenomenal, aspects of things that govern our daily lives will be lost to someone in such a state. In order to continue to live in the world and deal with its practical requirements, one must return from the state of mystic communication with the One to an everyday consciousness of discrete entities. In so doing, one again perceives from an individual viewpoint, and having such an individual or **self**-centered viewpoint implies having personal interests or desires.

Robert G. Henricks, *Lao-Tzu Te-Tao Ching*, p. 188, finds interpretations like mine "untenable given all that Lao-tzu says about desires and the need to lessen them or eliminate them in the rest of the book." It is easy to have desires — in fact it is practically impossible to avoid them. So most of Lao Zu's attention is indeed focused upon the need to learn to put them aside, which is the need to learn the techniques of deep trance. But in this key passage, with its emphasis on the duality of the noumenal and phenomenal aspects of the universe, he reserves a place of importance for desires. If one did not keep one foot in sthe normal human world, then one would be like the strange characters in the *Zhuang Zi* who wander around without being aware that they have a human identity.

第二章

天下皆知美之爲美，斯¹惡已。
皆知善之爲善，斯不善已。
故有無相生，難易相成，
長短相〈較〉〔形²〕，高下相傾，
音聲³相和，前後相隨。
是以聖人處無爲之事，
行不言之教。
萬物作焉而不辭，生而不有，
爲而不恃，功成而弗居。
夫唯弗居，是以不去。

2.

Everyone in the world knows the beautiful to be beautiful. Thus¹ there is ugliness. They all know good to be good. Thus there is evil. For being and non-being are mutually produced. Difficult and easy are mutually complemented. Long and short are mutually formed.² High and low are mutually opposed. Music and voice³ mutually harmonize. Fore and aft follow each other. For this reason, the Sage engages only in affairs that involve no active doing, and carries forth a wordless teaching. The myriad creatures arise and he does not deny any of them. They are produced, yet he does not seek to possess them. He acts and yet does not claim compensation for so doing. When he brings meritorious work to completion he takes no credit for it. For only by not taking credit for these accomplishments are the fruits of his activities kept safe.

NOTES:

1. Most translators and commentators take *si* 斯 in its weak sense as a demonstrative pronoun. But the argument presented in the text is clearly that opposites are mutually produced. There being one of a pair of opposites, the other must **thus** be called into existence.

2. Changed from *jiao* 較 in agreement with many texts. See Jiang Xi-chang, *Lao Zi Jiao-gu*, p. 13.

3. "Music" is the second dictionary definition for *sheng* 聲. The term refers to sounds produced by agitating various physical systems. *Yin* 音 is defined as a synonym for *sheng* but more specifically relates to variations of pitch, timbre, etc. It also applies to human speech sounds. Many different interpretations have been given for this pair.

4. For according to the general principle elucidated in this chapter, to act in a willful way that went against the Dao would involve the production of a reaction opposite to one's original intent, by which one would tend to thwart oneself.

第三章

不尚賢，使民不爭；
不貴難得之貨，使民不爲盜；
不見可欲，使民心不亂。
是以聖人之治，
虛¹其心，實其腹，
弱其志，強其骨。
常使民無知無欲。
使夫智者不敢爲也。
爲無爲²，則無不治。

3.

"Do not elevate the worthies, so that the people shall not contend. Do not value scarce commodities, so that the people shall not become robbers. Do not display desirable things, so that minds shall not become disordered." For this reason, the governance of the Sage lies in voiding the minds of the people,[1] filling their bellies, weakening their ambitions, and strengthening their bones. The Sage always causes the people to have no knowledge and no desires, and causes the ones who do know not to dare to act. Because [the Sage] engages in non-activity,[2] there is nothing he fails to bring to order.

NOTES:

1. A mind that is void is one that is without prejudices or preconceptions.

2. "Non-activity" is explained in chapter 48 as a limit case in which one's efficiency, derived from acting in accord with the Dao, is so great that one performs no discernible action.

Commentary:

This chapter does not advocate a policy of enforced ignorance. Rather it aims at reducing delusions caused by artificial social values, opinion that poses as objective information, and the like.

第四章

道沖，而用之或不盈。
淵兮似萬物之宗。
挫其銳，解其紛，
和其光，同其塵。
湛[3]兮似或存。
吾不知誰之子，象帝[4]之先。

4.

The Dao is void, yet when put to use it would seem that it can not be filled up.[1] Abyss-like, it seems to be the ancestor of the myriad creatures. It dulls their sharpness, releases their tangles, harmonizes their brightness, and unites their dust.[2] It is deep-entering,[3] as though existing. I do not know whose progeny it is, but it images the state before God.[4]

NOTES:

1. It has an inexhaustible capacity to receive and accept things.

2. Dust signifies the common elements from which all humans are constituted, and symbolizes their essential commonality despite their differing aspirations and pretensions. The same sentence occurs in chapter 56.

3. This word, *zhan* 湛, has many meanings. The basic meaning is "to sink." It also means "to settle out and become clear," "filled with," "thick and rich," "deep," "deep and full-bodied," etc.

4. The term (or at least the sequence of words) *xiang di* 象帝 is one of the most bewildering in the whole book simply because it is found in no other context. *Xiang* are in general "foreshadowings" of things that in some murky way foretell their future existence, but here the term seems to be used as a verb, "to resemble, to image, to mirror."

第五章

天地不仁，以萬物爲芻狗；
聖人不仁，以百姓爲芻狗。
天地之間，其猶橐籥乎！
虛而不屈，動而愈出。
多言數窮，不如守中。

5.

Heaven and Earth are not benevolent. They take the myriad creatures to be straw dogs.[1] The Sage is not benevolent. He takes the common people to be straw dogs. The space between Heaven and Earth is like a bellows. It is void and yet does not collapse. The more it moves the more it sends out. An excess of talk [aimed at fathoming the universe] is fated to become impoverished. It is better to hold [it] inside.

NOTES:

1. The straw dogs are explained in the *Zhuang Zi*, 14:30/82 (30/82 of the way through the fourteenth chapter). Dogs made of straw were treated with great reverence during a ritual, and discarded casually afterwards.

第六章

谷神不死，是謂玄牝。
玄牝之門，是謂天地根。
綿綿若存，用之不勤。

6.

The valley spirit does not die. It is called the dark and mysterious female. The portal of the dark and mysterious female is called the root of heaven and earth. It has a kind of wispy continuity as though existing. Use it without exertion.[1]

NOTES:

1. "*Qin* 勤" means "to labor wholeheartedly at something," "to cause others to labor," and "wholeheartedly." But according to the Gao You 高誘 commentary on the *Huai-nan Zi* 淮南子, it can also mean "to exhaust." If it is to be interpreted that way, then the question would be whether this passage affirms that the valley spirit is not exhausted, or whether it means that the one who uses it is not exhausted. I prefer to retain the ordinary meaning of this character, as given in my translation, because the commentaries frequently give rough paraphrases rather than strict definitions of terms. They tend to say what they think the author **means** by a term, rather than merely explaining its dictionary meaning. Since that is what this gloss appears to me to be, there seems to be little reason for making a direct substitution of meanings based on the commentaries in the absence of any other justification for so doing.

第七章

天長地久。
天地所以能長且久者，
以其不自生，故能長生。
是以聖人後其身而身先，
外其身而身存。
非以其無私邪？故能成其私。

7.

Heaven is long-abiding and earth is everlasting. The reason that Heaven
and Earth are able to be long-abiding and everlasting is that they do not
themselves give birth.[1] So they are able to produce for a long time. For
that reason, the Sage puts himself in the background and so finds himself
in the fore; he puts himself aside and so he is preserved. Is it not because
he has no selfish goals that he is able to succeed in regard to his personal
needs?

NOTES:

1. In the ordinary course of events, one creature is diminished to create or augment
another. The universe, here called Heaven and Earth, is a closed system. It does not
produce anything outside of its own boundaries, so it loses nothing and thus
endures.

第八章

上善若水，水善利萬物而不爭，
處眾人之所惡，故幾於道。
居善地，心善淵，
與善仁，言善信，
〈正〉〔政¹〕善治，
事善能，動善時。
夫唯不爭，故無尤。

8.

The highest good is like water. Water is good at benefiting the myriad creatures and does not contend. It takes its position in the places people hate, and so it approximates to the Dao.

The site makes a residence good. Depth makes a mind good. Benevolence makes giving good. Trustworthiness makes words good. Being able to put things in order makes government good. Being able to make actual accomplishments makes activities good. Timeliness makes movements good.

Now only by not contending can there be the absence of animosity.

NOTES:

1. Here is one case where the Wang Bi 王弼 (226–249) text has only the phonetic portion of the modern character. Most other versions, which I follow, add the radical.

Commentary:

This chapter seems to fall in three separate parts. It may be, however, that the intent of the author was to say that the lowly "residence" of water is good, and that people ought to emulate water and not contend for high status.

第九章

持而盈之，不如其已；
揣而〈梲〉〔銳¹〕之，不可長保。
金玉滿堂，莫之能守；
富貴而驕，自遺其咎。
功成〈名遂〉身退²，
天之道〔哉³〕。

9.

To grasp at things and seek to fulfill them is not as good as letting them be finished. [The blade] that is tested and sharpened¹ cannot be long protected. If gold and jade fill one's halls no one can guard them successfully. Being proud because of wealth and noble status calls down its own retribution. The Way of Heaven is that when one's accomplishments have been made <and fame follows> one should retire from the scene.[2,3]

NOTES:

1. For this substitution, see Jiang, p. 50f.

2. There are many variants of this sentence. The general sense is clear. The recently discovered texts written on silk scrolls (called hereafter the "silk texts") and many others do not include the words "and fame follows," and their inclusion would not seem to be consonant with the general Daoist attitudes toward fame.

3. This character has traditionally been written 載 and treated as the first character of the following chapter. See the note given at that point. If it be added at the end of this chapter, it has only an exclamatory function and does not affect the meaning of the passage.

第十章

〈載¹〉 營² 魄抱一，能無離乎？
專氣致柔，能嬰兒乎？
滌除玄〈覽〉〔鑑³〕，能無疵乎？
愛民治國，能無〈知〉〔爲⁴〕乎？
天⁵門開闔，能〈無〉〔爲〕雌乎？
明白四達，能無〈爲〉〔知〕乎？
生之畜之。
生而不有，爲而不恃⁶，
長而不宰，是謂玄德⁷。

10.

Nurture the dark soul and embrace unity.[1,2] Can you do so without fail?
Focus the lifebreath, making it as supple as possible. Can you in so doing
be like an infant? In cleaning up the dark and mysterious vision, can you
be without defect?[3] In loving the people and ordering the kingdom, can
you be without forceful activity?[4] In the opening and closing of the portal
of heaven[5] can you play the female part? Although your awareness reaches
to all points, can you yet abstain from the use of knowledge?

Give birth to them, nurture them. And yet while giving birth to them do
not possess them, and while acting (i.e., nurturing) claim no credit.[6]
Though senior to them do not rule over them. This is called the dark and
mysterious virtue.[7]

NOTES:

1. This same word, *zai* 載, occurs in chapter 29 in some versions, where it means "to load on." That reading is supported by a similar sentence in the poem *"Yuan you* 遠遊*"* (Far Journey) in the *Chu Ci* 楚辭 (*Songs of the South*) collection. But others say that the first character in chapter 10 should really be the last character in chapter 9 so that each line in chapter 9 has four characters and rhymes, and so that all lines in this chapter also have four characters. If it belongs to the end of chapter 9, then it must be read as 哉, and serves there only as an exclamation.

2. According to the *Zhong Wen Da Ci Dian*, in other contexts *"ying* 營*"* refers to the feminine, negative, *yin*, lifebreath. *"Po* 魄*"* also refers to an *yin* phenomenon. Wing-tsit Chan (陳榮捷), *The Way of Lao Tzu*, thinks *"ying po"* refers to the composite of "heavenly and earthly aspects of the soul," but both characters in the text suggest the earthly or feminine side of the soul. If Chan is right, then *"ying"* might better be written 熒. (Another possibility is that the character 營 should be the *ying* found in Mathews' dictionary, entry 7465, which is the same character minus the element 呂. That *"ying"* means "bright.") Other authorities, such as D. C. Lau (劉殿爵) in his *Tao Te Ching* and Arthur Waley in *The Way and Its Power*, think *"ying"* is used as an adjective here, meaning "perplexed." In his *Lao Zi Da-jie,* Yan Ling-feng (嚴靈峰) notes two instances in which Wang Bi uses the expression *"xing po* 形魄*"* and believes that *"xing"* and *"ying"* were so close in pronunciation that one was written for the other. Bernard Karlgren's reconstructions of ancient pronunciations in his *Grammata Serica Recensa* (entries 808d, *g'ieng*, and 843a, *g'iweng*) support that hypothesis. The *Chu Ci* has the expression *"zai ying po* 載營魄*."* The *Bao-pu Zi* 抱朴子 has the expression *"zai ying* 載營*."* (See Yan, p. 41.) Both of those expressions could have derived from this passage, so they cannot be used to establish anything definite about how these words should be understood here. Robert Henricks interprets *ying* to mean "to nourish," yielding the translation: "In nourishing the soul and embracing the One. . ." Since the lines parallel to this one all have, in one form or another, the general structure verb + object, and most have verb$_1$ object$_1$ verb$_2$ object$_2$, which is the way Henricks reads this sentence, it seems most likely that he is correct.

3. The Daoists believed the mind, in its perception of the world, functions like a mirror. Only a clean mirror can provide an undistorted view of the universe. The Wang Bi text has *lan* "vision" instead of *jian* "mirror." I follow the silk texts here.

4. My version in this and the following two lines agrees with the Tang dynasty text engraved on stone tablets (called hereafter the "stone version" or "stone text") in *Lao Zi Jiao-shi*. See also Yan Ling-feng's *Lao Zi Da-jie*, p. 42.

5. "Heaven" is a synonym for "nature." See Zhuang Zi's frequent use of the term in this sense. One instance is the beginning of chapter 6.

6. This sentence also occurs in chapters 2 and 51.

7. This sentence also occurs in chapter 51.

第十一章

三十輻，共一轂，
當其無，有車之用。
〈埏〉［摶²］埴以爲器，
當其無，有器之用。
鑿戶牖以爲室，
當其無，有室之用。
故有之以爲利，無之以爲用。

11.

Thirty spokes surround one hub. At that point of void[1] lies the utility of the cart. Mold[2] clay to make pots. In the void lies the functionality of the vessel. Fashion doors and windows in order to make a dwelling. In the void lies the functionality of the house. So what is substantial [in each case] provides the configuration,[3] and what is void provides the functionality.

NOTES:

1. Lit., to not have, and so, by extension, non-existence.

2. The Wang Bi text has *yan* ("boundary, limit"), whereas the intended meaning is clearly *tuan* ("roll around with the hand"). See Jiang, p. 64.

3. This meaning of *li* 利 is rare. See my *Explorations of Chinese Metaphysics* for a detailed study of this term.

Commentary:

A wheel with no hole for the axle to turn in would be useless, and a bowl with no hollow to hold liquids would serve no purpose. Of what use would a building with no entryway be?

第十二章

五色令人目盲；
五音令人耳聾；
五味令人口爽；
馳騁畋獵，令人心發狂；
難得之貨，令人行妨。
是以聖人爲腹，不爲目，
故去彼取此。

12.

The five colors blind people's eyes. The five notes of the scale deafen people's ears. The five flavors make people's palates go stale. Galloping about and hunting deranges people's minds. Scarce commodities make people do injurious deeds.[1] For this reason the Sage acts for the belly and not for the eyes. So he gets rid of that and takes this.[2]

NOTES:

1. Most scholars interpret this passage to mean that scarce commodities injure or impede the behavior or progress of people.

2. This sentence also occurs in chapters 38 and 72.

Commentary:

The belly indicates a kind of intuitive understanding, whereas the eyes indicate a kind of superficial knowledge.

第十三章

《寵辱若驚；〈貴[1]〉大患若身》。
何謂《寵辱若驚》？
寵〔之〕爲下[2,3]，
得之若驚，失之若驚，
是謂寵辱若驚。
何謂《〈貴〉大患若身》？
吾所以有大患者，爲吾有身，
及吾無身，吾有何患？
故貴〔以〕身於〔爲〕天下，
若可寄天下；
愛以身〔於〕爲天下，
若可託天下[4]。

13.

Favor and disgrace [both] produce alarm. A source of great travail is
one's self. What is meant by saying "Favor and disgrace produce alarm?"
He who is favored is someone's inferior.[2,3] Receiving favor and losing it
both cause alarm. That is what is meant by saying that "Favor and disgrace
produce alarm." What is meant by saying "A source of great travail is
one's self?" The reason I [can] have a great travail is that I have a self.
Should I no longer have a self then what travail could there be? So those
who take their selves as more valuable than ruling the world may be given
custody of the world. Those who love themselves more than ruling the
world may be entrusted with the world.[4]

NOTES:

1. Many authorities argue that *gui* 貴 is an intrusion in the text here. However, the Wang Bi text, the stone text, and the silk texts all have it. I have decided to delete it, not on the authority of others, but because I have finally reached the conclusion that only without it can the text be understood properly. The word *ruo* 若 is deliberately used in a different way in each of the first two sentences. In the first sentence *ruo* indicates that the first-mentioned things produce the second-mentioned thing. In the second sentence it indicates that the second-mentioned thing produces the first-mentioned thing. The two sentences thus form a kind of a play on words: Favor and disgrace produce —> alarm. A great travail produces <— having a "person," or a self, or an ego. The usual sentence order is inverted in the second sentence in Chinese. Or, if you prefer, the second *ruo* is used in a passive sense. (A great travail is produced by having a "person," or a self, or an ego.) If the sentence were written in the normal order it would be metrically awkward. Once again, there seems to be reason for believing that this text was originally passed down through the oral tradition. What is acceptable in writing may not be satisfying when recited. What is passable as poetry or song lyrics may offend one's sense of logic when written down. Probably the word *gui* was added because someone involved in the transmission of the text became confused by the odd syntax.

2. I have emended the text here. None of the attempts to explain this chapter that I have seen has been very successful. The A and B silk texts both have "寵之爲下," and that reading at least gives some hope of resolving the difficulties of this passage.

3. There are many variations in the above text. Some say "He who is favored is superior; he who is disgraced is inferior." But the silk text does not have anything about "the inferior." The ones that mention both "favor" and "disgrace" at this point are probably well-meaning emendations by someone who could not understand that one can only be "favored" by a superior, and so can suffer the misfortune of being in an inferior position. Of course, the author could have reported a commonplace observation — that one who is disgraced is also placed in an inferior position. But to do so would weaken the whole passage by stating the obvious.

4. The A and B silk texts both have: "故貴爲身於爲天下." In the next sentence, "愛以身爲天下," I believe that an originally present *yu* has already dropped out. "He who is more concerned with pursuing his own interests than with controlling the world can be entrusted with the world. He who loves his self more than controlling the world can be given safekeeping of the world." The *Zuan* 纂 text has: "貴以身於爲天下，則可以託天下。愛以身於爲天下，則可以寄天下。" "He who takes his own interests as more valuable than controlling the world can then be given safekeeping of the world. He who loves himself more than controlling the world can be entrusted with the world." In either case the saying is paradoxical since the author has just advised us that it is best *not* to have a self. But perhaps he means that it is even worse to strive to dominate the world.

第十四章

視之不見名曰夷，
聽之不聞名曰希，
搏之不得名曰微。
此三者不可致詰，故混而爲一。
其上不皦，其下不昧，
繩繩不可名，復歸於無物。
是謂無狀之狀，無物之象，
是謂惚恍。
迎之不見其首，隨之不見其後。
執古之道，以御今之有。
能知古始，是謂道紀。

14.

What eludes observation is called *yi* (level). What escapes hearing is called *xi* (silent). What cannot be grasped is called *wei* (minute). These three cannot be further pursued, so I meld them together as One. Its upper part is not bright. Its lower part is not dark. Unending, it cannot be adequately named and so returns to the status of nothingness. This is called the formless form, the image without a thing to be imaged. This is called impalpable and intangible. Going out to meet it we do not see its head. Following it we do not see its end. Grasp the Dao of antiquity to manage what is here today. Be able to know the ancient beginnings. [The chain from antiquity to the present] is called the Thread running through the Dao.

第十五章

古之善爲士者，微妙玄通，
深不可識。
夫唯不可識，故强爲之容。
豫〈焉〉〔兮¹〕若冬涉川，
猶兮若畏四鄰，
儼兮其若〈容〉〔客²〕，
渙兮若冰之將釋，
敦兮其若樸，
曠兮其若谷，
混兮其若濁。
孰能濁以靜之徐清，
孰能安以動之徐生。
保此道者不欲盈。
夫唯不盈，
故能〈蔽〉〔敝³〕〈不〉〔而⁴〕新成
。

15.

Those of old who were good at being knight-scholars were subtle, were possessed of ineffable efficacy, and were in dark and mysterious confluence, so profound that they could not be perceived. Only because they cannot be perceived do I give them a forced description. Cautious as though crossing a [frozen] stream in wintertime, apprehensive as though in fear of people on all four sides, deferential like a guest. Riven like ice on the verge of melting. Wholesome like the Uncarved Block.[5] Accepting like a valley. Turbid as though having been muddled. Who can be muddled in order to gradually become clear? Who can be tranquil in order that activity will gradually stir? Those who are protected in this Dao will not desire fullness. For only by not being full is one able to be tattered and yet newly complete.

NOTES:

1. Changed to be parallel with the following lines. The silk texts use a different character in this sentence and all the sentences parallel to it. Some texts leave this character out in this sentence and all the sentences parallel to it.

2. Changed on the basis of both meaning and rhyme. See Jiang, p. 90f.

3. At this point, the Wang Bi text writes a homonym for the character with the correct meaning.

4. I follow the emendation of Yi Shun-ding 易順鼎. See Yan Ling-feng, p. 62. The B silk text has "*bi er bu cheng*" at this point, "worn and not completed," as does one other version. See Jiang, p. 97f.

5. Chan notes: "It is not necessary to translate *p'u* literally as 'uncarved wood' or 'uncarved block' as Waley has done almost consistently. If any consistent translation is desired, it should be 'simplicity.'" But that term (*pu*) represents the true state of the universe and of the world of experience before human consciousness goes to work on it and fabricates (*zhi* 制) discrete entities out of it so that the limited human mind has something with which it can work. There is a clear need for a striking term to represent this concept in English.

第十六章

致虛極，守靜篤。
萬物並作，吾以觀〔其¹〕復。
夫物芸芸，各復歸其根。
歸根曰靜，是謂復命。
復命曰常。知常曰明。
不知常，妄作凶。
知常容，容乃公，公乃王，
王乃天，天乃道，道乃久。
沒身不殆。

16.

Promote the heights of vacuity. Preserve the wholesomeness of tranquility. The myriad creatures arise side by side, and [prepared by having maintained vacuity and tranquility] I observe their[1] recapitulations. For these creatures in profusion each return once more to their root. To return to the root is called tranquility, which in turn is called submitting again to Heaven's mandate.[2] Returning to Heaven's mandate is called being constant. Knowing the constant is called enlightenment. Should one not know the constant, one would wantonly commit evil deeds. By knowing the constant one can accept.[3] By accepting one is impartial. By being impartial one is kingly. By being kingly one is in concord with Heaven.[4] By being in concord with Heaven one is on the Dao. By being on the Dao one is long-lasting, and even though one should lose one's body one would not be endangered.

NOTES:

1. One character has been added in agreement with many versions.

2. *I.e.*, the inevitable.

3. *I.e.*, be tolerant.

4. *I.e.*, nature.

第十七章

太上，〈下〉〔不¹〕知有之；
其次，親而譽之；
其次，畏之；
其次，侮之。
信不足焉，有不信焉。
悠兮其貴言。
功成，事遂，百姓皆謂：
《我自然》。

17.

The people do not know that the Highest exists.[1] They praise and seek to get close to those on the next level. They fear those on the next level, and despise those on the level below that.

"When trust is inadequate there will be untrustworthiness."[2]

How remote[3] they appear in their (valuing words =) unwillingness to speak lightly. When their accomplishments come to fruition and events follow therefrom in their natural course, then the common people all say: "We did it of our own accord."

NOTES:

1. The Wang Bi text has *xia* 下 (the subordinates) instead of *bu* 不 (no, not). According to the Wang Bi text this line would be: "Their subjects know [only that] the Highest exists." Since the form of these two characters is so close, either might have been written in the earliest texts. The silk texts agree with the Wang Bi text, but I have chosen the other alternative (given in six versions) since all the phrases that follow in this sentence are pure predicates.

2. Appears also in chapter 23.

3. I follow the basic meaning of this word as given in the *Shuo Wen Jie Zi* 説文解字. The same definition is given in the Mao Heng 毛亨 commentary to the *Shi Jing* 詩經 recorded in Yan Ling-feng's *Lao Zi Da-jie*, p. 68.

第十八章

大道廢，有仁義；
智慧出，有大偽；
六親不和，有孝慈；
國家昏亂，有忠臣。

18.

When the great Dao is abandoned there then appear benevolence and righteousness. When intelligence and knowledge come into being there then appears great artifice. When the six kinds of kin are no longer in harmony then filial piety and parental compassion appear. When the realm is in disorder then there come to be loyal ministers.

第十九章

絕聖棄智，民利百倍；
絕仁棄義，民復孝慈；
絕巧棄利，盜賊無有。
此三者以爲文不足，故令有所屬。
見素抱樸，少私寡欲。
〔絕學無憂。¹〕

19.

Extirpate sageliness, discard wisdom, and the people will be benefited a hundredfold. Extirpate benevolence, discard righteousness, then the people will return to filial piety and parental compassion. Extirpate cleverness, discard profit, then robbers and thieves will be no more. The [foregoing] three [principles] are inadequately ornamented, and so I cause them to have [provisional maxims] under which they are subsumed: Display the Unbleached Fabric and embrace the Uncarved Block. Lessen selfish interests and decrease desires. [Extirpate study and have no worries.][1]

NOTES:

1. I agree with Henricks's arguments for moving this sentence back from the beginning of the next chapter.

第二十章

絕學無憂¹。
唯之與〈阿〉〔訶²〕，相去幾何？
善之與惡，相去若何？
人之所畏，不可不畏。
荒兮其未央哉！
眾人熙熙，如享太牢，如春登臺。
我獨泊兮其未兆，如嬰兒之未孩。
〈儽儽〉〔纍纍⁴〕兮，若無所歸。
眾人皆有餘，而我獨若遺。
我愚人之心也哉，沌沌兮！
俗人昭昭，我獨昏昏。
俗人察察，我獨悶悶。
澹⁵兮其若海，飂兮若無止。
眾人皆有以，而我獨頑且鄙。
我獨異於人，而貴食母。

20.

Extirpate study and there will no longer be worries.[1] What difference is there between a sound of compliance and angry rebuff?[2] How far is good from evil? "What people fear one cannot fail to fear." How wild and far off the mark! The multitudes are joyous as though partaking in the *tai-lao* sacrifice,[3] or as though ascending the terraces in springtime. I alone am placid like something before there is even an inkling of it, like an infant before it has learned to smile. Dispirited,[4] as though having no place to which to return. The multitudes all have an excess, and I alone seem to have a deficit. I have the mind of a stupid person, so chaotic. The ordinary people scintillate; I alone am muddled. The ordinary people are very prying, I alone am closed off. [They are] agitated like the sea, blown as if [they] would never stop.[5] The multitudes of people all have their goals. I alone am an obstinate fool and seem uncouth. I alone am different from others and value taking sustenance from the Mother.

NOTES:

1. If this line is not moved to the end of the previous chapter, then it seems appropriate to translate it in a slightly different way.

2. Most commentators and translators agree in making this substitution. The silk texts also have this meaning.

3. This sacrifice is one in which oxen, sheep, and pigs are offered at the altars to the spirits of land and grain (*she ji* 社稷).

4. The first character means "wearied," whereas the second character means "dispirited" and is more appropriate to the context.

5. *Dan* 澹 has two contrary meanings. I choose its basic meaning, although many translators chose the opposite meaning. *Liao* 飂 means "high wind," or (according to the Mathews dictionary) "wind in high places." It may also refer to the sound of the wind. It appears not to have any other meanings. The basic meaning of *dan* seems consonant with *liao*. Those who believe *dan* means "calm" here interpret the sentence to refer to the Daoist sage.

第二十一章

孔德之容，惟道是從。
道之爲物，惟恍惟惚。
惚兮恍兮，其中有象；
恍兮惚兮，其中有物。
窈兮冥兮，其中有精。
其精甚真，其中有信。
自古及今，其名不去，
以閱[1]衆甫。
吾何以知衆甫之然哉？以此。

21.

The greatest virtue's ability to accept follows only from the Dao. The Dao takes its guise as a creature only impalpably and intangibly. Intangible and impalpable, there are foreshadowings within it. Impalpable and intangible, there are creatures within it. Secluded and obscure, there is vitality within it. Its vitality is exceedingly genuine. Within it there is regularity. From antiquity down to the present its **true name** has never been cast aside, and so by means of that **true name** the progenitor of the multitudes is to be inspected.[1] How do I know the guises of the progenitor of the multitudes? By this.

NOTES:

1. This character, *yue* 閱, may originally have just been written *dui* 兑. It appears in some texts as *shuo* 説 or *yue* 悦 meaning "to enjoy." The basic meaning of *dui* is for the lips to crack open in a smile, which suggests not only the idea of "to

enjoy" for which *yue* 悦 is now usually written, but also the idea of something being given out from a storehouse. The *Zhong Wen Da Ci Dian* gives *bing* 稟 (to dispense, as from a government granary; to bestow) as the definition of *yue* in this passage, which meaning I was for a long time inclined to accept. The silk texts give *shun* 順 (*GSR*, 422d, *xiwen*), which according to Karlgren was not close in pronunciation either to *dui* 兑 (324a, *d'wâd*) or to its cognates. *Shun* is related in form and pronunciation to *xun* 巡 (462e, *dziwen*), which means "to inspect." One of the meanings of *yue* is "to inspect." Therefore, it seems possible that in the family of texts to which the silk texts belong someone wrote *shun* although it is *xun* that now represents the meaning he or she wanted to convey. If my understanding is correct, then once again the line of editors that produced the Wang Bi text succeeded in recording the correct character.

Commentary:

Note the prominence accorded to names by Lao Zi. In the first chapter, the "constant name" is given a position almost equal in prominence to the "constant way." Yan Ling-feng (p. 4) says it refers to the *ben zhen* 本真 of the universe, the fundamental verity of the universe, its apodictic even if ineffable characteristic of being. If we could say this "true name," we would name that which brings forth the multitudinous and self-propagating entities that are to be found in the universe. In normal consciousness, we are able to get only an imperfect experience of this name and whatever is behind it. This chapter seems to affirm that it is possible for some to experience the "progenitor of the multitudes."

第二十二章

曲則全，枉則直，窪則盈，
敝則新，少則得，多則惑。
是以聖人抱一為天下式。
不自見，故明。不自是，故彰。
不自伐，故有功。不自矜，故長。
夫唯不爭，故天下莫能與之爭。
古之所謂曲則全者，豈虛言哉？
誠全而歸之。

22.

"Crumpled then whole, twisted then straight, sunken-in then full, tattered then new, having little then acquiring much, having much then being made deluded" — for these reasons, the Sage embraces the One[1] to become the standard for the world. He does not show himself and so is luminous. He does not justify himself and so is illustrious. He does not boast of himself and so has merit. He does not brag on himself and so is senior to the rest. For only by his not being contentious does it happen that none in the world can contend with him. How could it have been empty words when the ancients said: "Crumpled then whole"? Verily such a one shall return whole to his source.[2]

NOTES:

1. Thereby avoiding these oppositions and the side effects that follow from them.

2. See Yan Ling-feng, *Lao Zi Da-jie*, p. 89, for his comments on a passage in the *Li Ji* 禮記 (*Book of Rites*) that refers to the moral duty of the child to return intact at death the body that his parents gave him intact at birth. The original passage is in the chapter called "Ji yi 祭義" (*Meaning of the Sacrifices*), 64/83.

第二十三章

希言自然。
故飄風不終朝，驟雨不終日。
孰爲此者？天地。
天地尚不能久，而況於人乎？
故從事於道者，道者同於道；
德者同於德；失者同於失。
同於道者，道亦樂得之；
同於德者，德亦樂得之；
同於失者，失亦樂得之。
信不足焉，有不信焉。

23.

To be taciturn is the way of nature. For a gale cannot last the whole morning. A torrential rain cannot last the entire day. What makes them? Heaven and Earth. How can humans make things endure for long when not even Heaven and Earth can do so? So in engaging in activities, those who act in accord with the Dao are akin to the Dao, those who act in accord with Virtue are akin to Virtue, and those who act in accord with Loss are akin to Loss. Those who act in accord with the Dao are welcomed by the Dao. Those who act in accord with Virtue are welcomed by Virtue. Those who act in accord with Loss are welcomed by Loss.

"When trust is inadequate, there will be untrustworthiness."[1]

NOTES:

1. Appears also in chapter 17.

第二十四章

企者不立，跨者不行，
自見者不明，自是者不彰，
自伐者無功，自矜者不長。
其在道也，曰：
餘食贅〈行〉〔形¹〕。
物或惡之，故有道者不處。

24.

Those who rise on tiptoe do not stand firm. Those who straddle as wide as possible cannot move. Those who show themselves off are not luminous. Those who justify themselves are not illustrious. Those who boast of themselves have no merit. Those who brag on themselves do not stand senior to others. In respect of the Dao, these [behaviors] are said to be leftovers and excrescences. Creatures always loathe them, and so those who have the Dao do not involve themselves therewith.

NOTES:

1. *Xing* 行 (to move, to travel) has been replaced with *xing* 形 (form) according to the *Pan* 潘 version. See Jiang, p. 163.

第二十五章

有物混成，先天地生。
寂兮寥兮，獨立〔而¹〕不改，
周行而不殆，可以爲天下母。
吾不知其名，
字之曰道，強爲之名曰大。
大曰逝，逝曰遠，遠曰反。
故道大，天大，地大，王亦大。
域中有四大，而王居其一焉。
人法地，地法天，天法道，
道法自然。

25.

There is a thing that was turbidly formed, born before Heaven and Earth. Solitary and vacant, it stands alone and unchanging. It reaches everywhere without falling into any danger. It can be the mother of the world. I know not its taboo name.² To serve as a name-for-outsiders I call it Dao, and if forced to provide a taboo name will call it the Great. Being great means going forward. Going forward means being far. Being far means turning back on itself. So the Dao is great, Heaven is great, Earth is great, and the king³ is also great. Within the domain there are four greats, and the king is one of them. Humans model themselves on Earth, Earth models itself on Heaven, Heaven models itself on the Dao, and the Dao models itself on what is as it is in itself.⁴

NOTES:

1. Added to maintain this sentence's structure parallel to that of the next sentence. See Jiang, p. 167.

2. The same term is translated elsewhere as "true name." Presumably the view was that if one knows and uses the true name of someone else, one gains magical power over him, and so the use of the name should be tabooed.

3. Some texts have "people" instead of "king."

4. This is the universe that does not give birth to anything beyond itself. See chapter 7.

第二十六章

重爲輕根，
靜爲躁君。
是以
聖人終日行，
不離輜重，
〈雖〉〔唯¹〕有〈榮觀〉〔環館²〕，
〈燕〉〔宴³〕處超然。
奈何萬乘之主，
而以身輕天下？
輕則失〈本〉〔根⁴〕，
躁則失君。

26.

Heaviness is the root of lightness. Tranquility is the ruler of agitation. For this reason, the Sage travels all day without departing from his heavy-framed vehicle. Only when there are encircling way stations does he reside at his ease in seclusion. How can a ruler of a myriad chariots treat himself with levity compared to the [things of the] world? If one [abandons oneself to] levity then one loses one's roots, and if one becomes agitated then one will lose one's autonomy.

NOTES:

1. Corrected according to the A silk text. See Henricks, p. 238, the note on his line four.

2. Corrected according to the A and B silk texts. The ancient pronunciations of *guan* 觀 and *guan* 官 were almost identical, and the latter was apparently written for *guan* 館. The ancient pronunciations of *rong* 榮 and *huan* 環 are similar. See Karlgren, *Grammata Serica Recensa,* entries 157a, 157k, 158i, 256n, and 843d. I accept the interpretations of this passage by Henricks and Lau.

3. The first character is a homonym written for the second character.

4. I have put the text into pairs of rhyming lines. It appears that the fourth character of the last line was miswritten at some time and later corrected to root (*ben* 本) on the basis of the meaning of the passage. In some versions it was changed to minister (*chen* 臣) on the basis of rhyme and because the parallel structure of the line suggested that in one case one might lose a minister and in another case one might lose a ruler (*jun* 君). See Jiang, p. 177.

第二十七章

善行無轍跡，
善言無瑕讁，
善數不用籌策，
善閉無關鍵而不可開，
善結無繩約而不可解。
是以聖人常善救人，故無棄人；
常善救物，故無棄物。
是謂〈襲〉［習1］明。
故善人者，不善人之師；
不善人者，善人之資。
不貴其師，不愛其資，
雖智大迷。是謂要妙。

27.

Good traveling leaves no ruts. Good speech gives rise to no reproach. Good reckoning does not depend on counting slips. Good closures need no bars and yet cannot be opened. Good bonds employ no rope and yet cannot be undone.

For this reason the Sage is always good at saving people and so none is abandoned. He is always good at saving creatures and so none is abandoned. [This condition] is called practicing[1] brightness. So the good person is the teacher of those who are not good, and people who are not good are the raw materials for those who are good. Should one fail to value his teacher or fail to love his raw materials, then although he might be knowledgeable, he would yet be greatly deluded. This is spoken of as the cardinal mystery.[2]

NOTES:

1. The ancient pronunciations of *xi* 襲 and *xi* 習 were almost identical, which explains why the first could be written for the second. Confirmation of the meaning "to practice" is offered by the silk texts' use of two characters that are apparently corruptions of yi 愶, a character that also means "to practice." See Lau, p. 306. Yan Ling-feng's suggestion that *xi ming* 襲明 means "shrouded brightness," while ingenious, does not seem to be correct in view of the characters chosen by the silk text scribes. (See Yan, p. 110ff.)

2. *Miao,* inexplicable efficacy.

第二十八章

知其雄，守其雌，爲天下谿。
爲天下谿，常德不離，
復歸於嬰兒。
知其白，守其黑，爲天下式。
爲天下式，常德不忒，
復歸於無極。
知其榮，守其辱，爲天下谷。
爲天下谷，常德乃足，復歸於樸。
樸散則爲器，聖人用之，
則爲官長。
故大制不割。

28.

Know the male, but keep to the female and be thus a valley to the world. When one is a valley to the world, the constant virtue will not desert one and one will return to the state of being an infant. Know the white but keep to the black and be thus a model to the world. If one is a model to the world, then the constant virtue will not decline and one will return to the limitless. Know glory but keep to disgrace and so be a valley to the world. If one is a valley to the world then constant virtue will be sufficient and one will return to the Uncarved Block. When the Uncarved Block is cut asunder it then becomes utensils. [But] should a Sage use such a man,[1] that person would become a senior official. Truly, great fabrication does not involve cutting.[2]

NOTES:

1. This phrase is clear in the traditional text. "The sage uses it." But the "it" is not present in the silk texts, leading both Lau and Henricks to translate it as a passive construction — When the sage is used. But why speak of sundering the pure simplicity of the Uncarved Block to make an official, and then say that really great work is only accomplished when such sundering is not committed? It seems that the traditional text implies that when a sage uses a man he does so in such a way that the man is not alienated from the Uncarved Block. Neither Henricks nor Lau have adduced arguments for translating a sentence of the simple form "noun + verb" as a passive utterance.

2. I follow Waley, p. 178, who has one way out of the non sequitur this passage seems to involve: He points out that zhi 制 has the surface meaning of "fabricate" here, but also can mean "to regulate, to govern." So he says that "the secondary meaning is that the greatest ruler does the least chopping about."

第二十九章

將欲取天下而爲之，
吾見其不得已。
天下神器，不可爲也，
爲者敗之，執者失之。
故物或行或隨，或歔或吹，
或强或羸[1]，
或〈挫〉〔培[2]〕或隳。
是以聖人去甚，去奢，去泰。

29.

Should one desire to take the world and control it, I see that there would
be no end [to one's involvement]. The world is a holy vessel and cannot be
controlled. Those who try to control it harm it. Those who clutch at it lose
it. For some things go before and some things follow. Some things snort
and some things blow. Some things are strong and some things are puny.
Some things are nurtured and others are destroyed.[2] For that reason the
Sage gets rid of extremes, extravagances, and excesses.[3]

NOTES:

1. Many texts write *ying* 嬴 by mistake. *Lei* 羸 means "weak" whereas *ying* means
"to win."

2. The two terms in the previous phrase, "strong" and "puny," are opposites. But
in this phrase the original text had *cuo* 挫, which means "to push down" and other
negative meanings that do not form a good contrast to *hui* 隳, which means "to

destroy." Three alternatives, 陪 、 培 、 坏, are pronounced *pei*, two sharing a phonetic component, and a third having a phonetic component (不) that looks much like the original form of the aforementioned phonetic component (高   =? 咼). Of these, the first means "to accompany," the second means "to nurture," and the third means "earthenware that has not yet been fired." It seems clear that these three were written down on the basis of their sound. A fourth alternative, *zai* 載, may have been supplied by someone because that character shares one meaning with *pei* 培. See Jiang, p. 75. A fifth alternative, *jie* 接, is similar in visual form to *pei* 培. Once again we see indications of people writing out a text from memory, and frequently struggling to remember the correct characters.

3. The sage avoids extremes because they invariably carry the pendulum to the end of its arc, storing up much potential energy in the process, and inevitably leading to an irresistible swing back in the other direction.

第三十章

以道佐人主者，不以兵强天下。
其事好還。
師之所處，荊棘生焉。
大軍之後，必有凶年。
善者果而已，不敢以取强。
果而勿矜，果而勿伐，果而勿驕。
果而不得已，果而勿强。
物壯則老，是謂〈不〉〔否²〕道。
〈不〉〔否〕道早已。

30.

Those who use the Dao to aid the masters of men do not employ weapons to take the world by force. That tactic is good at recoiling upon its origin. Where armies have trodden, thorns and brambles spring up. After the great armies there must follow bad years. In the case of good use of armies, they are employed only until results are obtained, and nobody dares use them to grab power. When results are obtained, they dare not brag. When results are obtained, they dare not boast. When results are obtained, they dare not be arrogant. When results are obtained, it is solely because there was no other way out. When results are obtained, they do not try to dominate. — When creatures come to their prime, they begin to age. That[1] is spoken of as the dao (course) of retrograde action.[2] What is on the retrograde dao is soon finished.

NOTES:

1. "That" refers to any of the above choices that comes to an analogous state of fulfillment and so is to be avoided. For example, after a successful *defensive* war, to go on to seek domination is analogous to coming to one's prime as a nation. From there on everything must be downhill because the burgeoning power of growth has been capped off. This passage gives another example of the rebound phenomenon mentioned in the previous chapter.

2. See Yan Ling-feng's *Lao Zi da-jie*, p. 125, for a discussion of this "course of retrograde action." Besides being similar in form, the ancient pronunciations of *bu* 不 and fou 否 were the same. (See Karlgren, *Grammata Serica Recensa*, entries 999a and 999e.) Yan Ling-feng notes that two versions of the text write fei 非 instead of 不, which indicates some variability in the text at this point. The ordinary modern pronunciation of 否 is *fou*, but its alternate modern pronunciation, which applies to its meaning in this passage, is *pi*. Whether 否 had an ancient second pronunciation that was closer to that of 非, I have not yet determined.

In any event, it is the meaning of 否 used in the twelfth hexagram of the *Yi Jing* (*Book of Changes*) that is relevant here, as Yan demonstrates. The *pi* hexagram, consisting of three broken lines surmounted by three unbroken lines, depicts the departure of the upper "great" lines in the face of the arrival of the lower "petty" lines. "Thus," as Legge translates, "the way of the small man appears increasing, and that of the superior man decreasing." That state could only prevail when the status and activity of the superior men has been too much in the ascendant. Hence it is appropriate that "the superior man . . . restrain [the manifestation of] his virtue, and avoid the calamities [that threaten him]."

Pi does not mean "stopped up" or "capped off" in the usual sense that something is opposing, negating, or impeding one's progress. Rather, it means that something is pushing one from behind so irresistibly that there is no alternative to "going around the bend" and then to continue being pushed by the force of events in the opposite direction. It is motion negated — not in the sense of being stopped dead, but in the sense of going in the direction that is mathematically negative to the original direction.

第三十一章

夫佳兵者不祥之器，物或惡之，
故有道者不處。
君子居則貴左，用兵則貴右。
兵者不祥之器，非君子之器，
不得已而用之，恬淡爲上。
勝而不美，而美之者，是樂殺人。
夫樂殺人者，
則不可以得志於天下矣。
吉事尚左，凶事尚右。
偏將軍居左，上將軍居右。
言以喪禮處之。
殺人之眾，以哀悲泣之，
戰勝以喪禮處之。

31.

Excellent weapons are inauspicious instruments. Creatures always abhor them. So those who have the Dao do not become involved with them. When the ruler resides at peace he values the left, and when he takes up arms he values the right. Arms are inauspicious instruments, not instruments fit for a noble man. Only when there is no alternative does he resort to them. [And then] placidity and blandness are the best. He does not regard victory as glorious. Those who glorify victory exult in killing people. Now those who exult in killing people cannot achieve their aspirations in this world. For auspicious affairs one elevates the left. For inauspicious affairs one elevates the right. The lieutenant generals take their stations on the left. The full generals reside on the right.[1] [Because the right is the side of mourning, the above discussion] means that one ought to treat [military] affairs with the rites of mourning. Because of the large numbers of people who are killed, they are to be wept for with sorrow. Victory in war should be treated with the rites of mourning.[2]

NOTES:

1. Chan, p. 155, says that "the terms 'lieutenant general' and 'senior general' . . . did not appear until Han times." Lin Yutang makes the same observation. If this statement is true, then both silk texts must have been copied during the Han dynasty since they both employ these terms.

2. See Waley's translation of the material from the *Yi Zhou Shu* 逸周書, 32, on p. 250 of *The Way and Its Power*.

第三十二章

道常無名，樸雖小，
天下莫能臣也。
侯王若能守之，萬物將自賓。
天地相合，以降甘露，
民莫之令而自均。
始制[1]，有名，
名亦既有，夫亦將知止，
知止〈可〉〔所[2]〕以不殆。
譬道之在天下，
猶川谷之〈於〉〔與[3]〕江海。

32.

The Dao is always nameless. Although the Uncarved Block is small, nothing in the world can subordinate it. If the lords and kings can hold fast to it, then the myriad creatures will come to be their vassals of their own accord.

Heaven and Earth will couple in order to let the sweet dew fall. Although no people shall so command, the [distribution of sweet dew] will be equitable of its own accord.

Only after fabrication occurs are there names,[1] and once there are names people ought to know where to stop, for by knowing where to stop they can escape danger.

For example, the Dao in relation to the world is like the way the streams and valleys supply [water to] the rivers and oceans.

NOTES:

1. Compare with chapter 28.

2. Many texts, including the silk texts, differ from Wang Bi's version. See Jiang, p. 219.

3. Many texts, including the silk texts, have this version. Wang Bi's commentary also follows this version. See Jiang, p. 220.

Commentary:

This passage falls into four seemingly unconnected passages. The A and B silk texts are no better. Chan agrees with Hu Shi that the second passage above does not rhyme with the rest of the lines in this chapter and that its meaning is not consistent with the rest of the chapter either. Eliminating it would make a closer connection between what is now the first passage and the third, but the fourth passage would still be disconnected.

第三十三章

知人者智，自知者明。
勝人者有力，自勝者強。
知足者富，強行者有志。
不失其所者久，死而不亡者壽。

33.

Those who know other people are knowledgeable. Those who know themselves are enlightened. Those who overcome other people are forceful. Those who overcome themselves are strong. Those who know when they have enough are rich. Those who act strongly have aspirations. Those who do not lose their positions are long enduring. Those who die and yet do not perish have life everlasting.[1]

NOTES:

1. The silk texts have *wang* 忘 (to forget) instead of *wang* 亡 (to perish), so some authorities say this sentence means that those who "live long" are those who die and yet are not forgotten.

第三十四章

大道氾兮，其可左右。
萬物恃之而生而不辭，
功成〈不名有〉〔而不有[1]〕，
衣養萬物而不爲主。
常無欲，可名於小；
萬物歸焉而不爲主，可名爲大。
以其終不自爲大，故能成其大。

34.

The great Dao reaches everywhere without regard to direction. The myriad creatures depend on it to reproduce themselves and be born, and not one is denied. When accomplishments are made [the Dao] does not claim them. It feeds and clothes the myriad creatures and does not act as their master. Constantly without desire [in regard of the myriad creatures] it can be called insignificant. The myriad creatures take refuge therein and yet it does not act as their master, so it can be called great. Because it never takes itself to be great it can therefore accomplish its own greatness.

NOTES:

1. Emended according to Jiang, p. 225.

第三十五章

執大象，天下往。
往而不害，安平太。
樂與餌，過客止。
道之出〈口〉〔言¹〕，
淡乎其無味，
視之不足見，聽之不足聞，
用之不足既。

35.

Grasp the great Image and [all in] the world will approach. They approach
and are not injured, thus great is their peace and tranquility. When there is
music and food, the passing travellers will stop in. [But] the Dao when
expressed in words[1] is found bland and flavorless, when looked at
provides nothing to see, when listened to provides nothing to hear. [Yet]
when put into use, there is no way to exhaust it.

NOTES:

1. The text Wang Bi used apparently originally had *yan* 言 here, as do several
other texts including the silk texts. *Yan* rhymes with the rest of the chapter,
whereas *kou* 口 does not. See Jiang, p. 233f. See also, Karlgren, *Grammata
Serica Recensa,* entries 110a, 241a, 251a, 441f, 515c, and 531g.

第三十六章

將欲歙之，必固張之。
將欲弱之，必固強之。
將欲廢之，必固興之。
將欲奪之，必固與之。
是謂微明。柔弱勝剛強。
魚不可脫於淵，
國之利器不可以示人。

36.

If one would contract something, then one must first resolutely spread it out. If one would weaken something, then one must first resolutely strengthen it. If one would have a thing be discarded, one must first resolutely cause it to flourish. If one would seize something one must first resolutely give it away. This [approach] is called subtle discernment. The pliant and weak overcome the rigid and strong. [So] fish cannot leave the depths and the sharp instruments of the state cannot be shown [to threaten] the people.[1,2]

NOTES:

1. See R. B. Blakney's note calling attention to the relation between this line and the *Zhuang Zi*, where the same line occurs at 10:21/41. See also Waley's note calling attention to a related passage in the *Yi Zhou Shu* 逸周書, chapter 52.

2. The *Lao Zi* says this because the fish and the weapons are rigid and strong things that will quickly perish when removed from their supporting medium. As fish must be submerged in water to survive, so weapons must be kept in concealment rather

than being removed from their sheaths and turned against the people. In fact, the people themselves would seem to be analogous to the waters that conceal the fish. So probably the author of these lines means that the weapons belong with the people. That is to say, they should belong to the people and not to professional soldiers who may try to oppress the people.

第三十七章

道常無爲而無不爲，
侯王若能守之，萬物將自化。
化而欲作，吾將鎮之以無名之樸。
無名之樸，夫亦將無欲。
不欲以靜，天下將自定。

37.

The Dao never employs forceful action yet there is nothing it fails to do.
If the lords and rulers can hold to it, then the myriad creatures will
transform themselves of their own accord. Should desire rise up [even]
after they have transformed, I will tranquilize it with the nameless
Uncarved Block. [By reason of] the nameless Uncarved Block, the [myriad
creatures] too will in future become desireless. Their having been stilled
by desirelessness, the world will become settled of its own accord.

Commentary:

The ancient Ma-Wang Dui texts are substantially different: "The Dao is always
nameless. If the lords and rulers are able to hold to it, then the myriad creatures will
transform of their own accord. Should they transform and [yet] rise up I will
tranquilize them. Tranquilize them with the nameless Uncarved Block. By means of
the Uncarved Block. Now in future they will not be insulted. Because they will not
be insulted they will be tranquil, and Heaven and Earth will in future set themselves
to rights."

第三十八章

上德不德，是以有德；
下德不失德，是以無德。
上德無爲而無以爲；
〈下德爲之而有以爲；²〉
上仁爲之而無以爲；
上義爲之而有以爲。
上禮爲之而莫之應，
則攘臂而扔之。
故失道而後德，失德而後仁，
失仁而後義，失義而後禮，
夫禮者忠信之薄，而亂之首。
前識者，道之華，而愚之始。
是以大丈夫處其厚，不居其薄，
處其實，不居其華。
故去彼取此。

38.

The highest virtue is not virtuous and for that reason has [true] virtue. The lesser virtue does not lose virtue and for that reason does not have [true] virtue. The highest virtue does not engage in [forceful] activity and so uses nothing to do things.¹ <The lesser virtue does things and uses something to do so.²> The highest benevolence does things and does so by means of nothing. The highest righteousness does things and does so by means of something. The highest propriety does things and if nothing responds to what it does then it thrusts out its forearms and forces them. So after the Dao is lost, there is virtue. After virtue is lost, there is benevolence. After benevolence is lost, there is righteousness. After righteousness is lost, there is propriety. Now propriety is the husk of faithfulness and trust and the beginning of disorder. The initial discernments[3] are the detritus[4] of the Dao and the beginnings of ignorance. For this reason the great man abides in the substantial parts and does not tarry in the husk. He abides in the solid parts and does not tarry in the detritus. So he rejects that and accepts this.

NOTES:

1. Most interpreters believe that when it speaks of "using nothing" the text refers to depending on no set ideas or intentions. When it next speaks of "using something" it means that there are such set ideas or intentions present in mind to motivate action. Viewed somewhat more cynically, these mental states could be called ulterior motives.

2. This phrase is in neither the A or B silk text. Its presence disturbs the otherwise very regular change of multiple attributes from the highest virtue or power to mere propriety. Note that there is no mention of a "lesser benevolence," "lesser righteousness," or "lesser propriety." I believe that some early redactor in seeking to improve the text actually added an extraneous element. Henricks makes the same observation, p. 98.

3. Lit., ones who first perceive, or ones who are first perceived.

4. I translate *hua* 華 (blossom —> efflorescence) as "detritus." This *hua* is a cognate of the word *hua* 花 that means "flower." (In fact, the latter character does not appear to have been in use until the Northern Dynasties period.) But as a verb, the latter term also means for something to dissipate, to lose ability to focus and so see in a blurred way, to become diffuse in outline, as when an aspirin pill dropped

in water begins to dissolve. This meaning seems to derive from the observation that flowers, which have relatively soft outlines, come from compact and sharply defined buds. When a bar of some substance begins to corrode, deposits of oxide may accumulate on the surface of the bar and muddle its formerly clear-cut outline. So the *hua* of something may refer to its state after it has begun to decompose.

3. The *Mencius*, 3A:5, speaks of how those who first come to awareness of moral verities should bring others to the same awareness.

Commentary:

Perhaps the transition is from goallessness to goalfulness to arbitrary exactions?

第三十九章

昔之得一者，
天得一以清，地得一以寧，
神得一以靈，谷得一以盈，
萬物得一以生，
侯王得一以爲天下〈貞〉〔正[1]〕。
其致之〔一也[2]〕。
天無以清將恐裂，
地無以寧將恐發（廢[3]），
神無以靈將恐歇，
谷無以盈將恐竭，
萬物無以生將恐滅，
侯王無以貴高將恐蹶。
故貴以賤爲本，高以下爲基。
是以侯王自謂孤、寡、不穀，
此非以賤爲本邪？非乎？
故致數[4]譽無譽[5,6]。
不欲琭琭如玉，珞珞[7]如石。

39.

Of those in ancient times who attained unity: Heaven attained unity in
order to be pure. Earth attained unity in order to be stable. Spirits attained

unity in order to be responsive. The valleys attained unity in order to be full. The myriad creatures attained unity in order to reproduce. The lords and kings attained unity in order to become the correct ones in the world.[1] [It is unity that][2] brings them to this height. If Heaven did not have what it takes to be pure, it would probably become rent. If Earth did not have the means to be stable, it would probably quake.[3] If the spirits did not have the means to be responsive, they would probably dissipate. If the valleys did not have the means to be filled, they would probably become exhausted. If the myriad creatures did not have the means to reproduce, they would probably become extinct. If the lords and kings did not have the means to be noble and exalted, they would probably fall. So the noble takes the ignoble as its base, and the high takes the low as its foundation. For this reason the lords and kings speak of themselves as the orphaned, the bereaved, and the unworthy. Is this not taking the ignoble as one's base? Is this not so? So the highest degree[4] of good repute is to have no good repute.[5,6] Be not glistening like jade [but] stony[7] like rock.

NOTES:

1. For this emendation, see Jiang, p. 253f.

2. For the addition of these two characters, see Jiang, p. 255, and Yan Ling-feng, p. 169.

3. The character *fa* 發 is probably a mistake for *fei* 廢. The first character means to shoot off (arrows), and the second means for a house (or other object) to be destroyed. The two words are probably cognates, the idea of destruction following from the idea of being "shot off" to impact or crash at some other point. See Jiang, p. 255, for corroborative evidence.

4. Reading 數 as *shu*, this character is explained as meaning "most" or "highest."

5. The Wang Bi commentary and fifteen other versions have this reading, which is also confirmed by both silk texts.

6. This sentence is a good example of how the oldest texts were written with characters that were still fluid in form. The A silk text has *yu* 與, the B silk text has *yu* 輿, but neither is really the correct character. Context shows the correct character to be *yu* 譽. But some texts even give *ju* 車. According to Karlgren's reconstruction of the Ancient Chinese pronunciations of these characters, the first three were almost identical and the last had an additional initial consonant. See his entries in *Grammata Serica Recensa,* 89b, 89i, 89j, and 74a.

7. Alternatives for the first of these two words include: 琭 、 碌 、 祿 、 錄. The compound 碌碌 is descriptive of glistening stone. See Gao Shu-fan, p. 1156. Alternatives for the second word include: 珞 、 落 、 硌. The compounds 珞珞 and 落落 are defined as the roughness of stone. Many authorities follow the He-shang Gong 河上公 commentary and say that these two terms refer to the scarcity of jade and the commonness of rocks. Many translations use strained interpretations such as "the tinkling of jade and the rumble of stones" for which I have not found support in any dictionary or commentary.

第四十章

反（返）者道之動；弱者道之用。
天下萬物生於有，有生於無。

40.

Recirculation is [characteristic of] the motion of the Dao. Weakness is [characteristic of] the functioning of the Dao. The myriad creatures of the world are produced out of things that exist.[1] Existence is produced from non-existence.[1]

NOTES:

1. Lit., "what there is" and "what there isn't."

第四十一章

上士聞道，勤而行之；
中士聞道，若存若亡；
下士聞道，大笑之。
不笑，不足以爲道。
故建言有之：
明道若昧，進道若退，
夷道若纇，上德若谷，
大白若辱，廣德若不足，
建德若偷，質〈真〉〔德¹〕若渝，
大方無隅，
大器晚成，大音希聲，
大象無形，道隱無名。
夫唯道，善貸且〔善³〕成。

41.

When the superior knight-scholar hears of the Dao, he diligently puts it
into practice. When the average knight-scholar hears of the Dao, it is half
as though he preserves [the concept of] it in his mind and half as though it
is lost. When the inferior knight-scholar hears of the Dao, he laughs
uproariously at the notion. If such a one did not laugh at it, it would be
something too inadequate to be the Dao. So an established saying states that
the brightness of the Dao seems like darkness, the advance of the Dao
seems like retreat, the level Dao seems rough, the superior virtue seems

like a gully, the whitest white seems sullied, ample virtue seems inadequate, firmly established virtue seems stealthy, pristine virtue seems polluted, the greatest square has no corners, the greatest vessels are completed late,[2] the greatest sound is inaudible, the greatest image has no form. The Dao hides itself in namelessness. Now only the Dao is good at bestowing [things upon the creatures of the world] and bringing [them] to completion.

NOTES:

1. See Jiang, p. 276, for the addition of this character.

2. Lin Yutang's translation says that "great talent takes long to mature," which is surely the intended meaning of this sentence.

3. See Jiang, p. 278f, for the addition of this character.

第四十二章

道生一，一生二，
二生三，三生萬物。
萬物負陰而抱陽，沖氣以爲和。
人之所惡，唯孤、寡、不穀，
而王公以爲稱。
故物或損之而益，或益之而損。
人之所教，我亦教之，
強梁者不得其死，
吾將以爲教父。

42.

The Dao produced the One. The One produced the Two. The Two produced the Three. And the Three produced the myriad creatures. The myriad creatures bear Yin on their backs and embrace Yang. They blend lifebreaths in order to create a harmony. People abominate nothing more than to be orphaned, bereaved, and unworthy, yet the lords and kings take these [terms] as their appellations. So creatures may be worn away and thereby augmented, or they may be augmented and thereby worn away.

What other people teach I also teach: "Ruffians will come to no good end." I take this as my precept.

第四十三章

天下之至柔，馳騁天下之至堅，
無有入無間。
吾是以知無爲之有益。
不言之敎，無爲之益，
天下希及之。

43.

The most pliant things in the world ride roughshod over the hardest.
Non-being enters even where there is no fissure. For this reason I know
the benefit of non-action. Few in the world can attain to [comprehension
of] the wordless teaching or to the benefits of non-activity.

第四十四章

名與身孰親？
身與貨孰多？
得與亡孰病？
是故甚愛必大費，多藏必厚亡。
知足不辱，知止不殆，可以長久。

44.

Which is dearer to you, your [good] name or your life? Which [counts] more with you, your person or your material goods? Which is the more injurious, gain or loss? For these reasons, extreme love must involve great costs and great accumulations must involve heavy losses. Knowing when you have enough [means] no ignominy, and knowing when to stop [means] no danger, so one can long endure.

第四十五章

大成若缺，其用不〈弊〉〔敝¹〕；
大盈若沖，其用不窮。
大直若屈，大巧若拙，大辯若訥。
躁勝寒，靜勝熱，清靜爲天下正。

45.

The greatest accomplishment seems to have imperfections, yet there is no impairment in its function. The greatest fullness is like vacuity, yet in use it is never exhausted. The greatest straightness is like crookedness. The greatest knack is like clumsiness. The greatest eloquence is like stumbling speech. Agitation overcomes the cold, and tranquility overcomes the heat. The pure and tranquil are the correct ones in the world.

1. The *bi* that means "malpractice, corruption" is mistakenly written for the *bi* that means "worn out."

第四十六章

天下有道，卻走¹馬以糞；
天下無道，戎馬生於郊²。
〔罪莫大於可欲。³〕
禍莫大於不知足；
咎莫大於欲得。
故知足之足，常足矣。

46.

When the Dao prevails in the world, fleet-footed horses[1] are turned back
[to the fields] in order to fertilize them. When the Dao does not prevail in
the world, war horses are foaled in the outskirts of the cities.[2] [There is no
greater transgression than condoning desire.[3]] There is no greater disaster
than failing to know when you have enough. There is no greater
retribution than acquisitiveness. So the adequacy of knowing when you
have enough is [itself] a constant adequacy.

NOTES:

1. "*Zou* 走" literally means "to run, to gallop." I think this sort of horse is more
general in its characteristics than the war horses mentioned in the next line, and
probably included horses intended for use in the hunt and for delivering messages.
At any time before the very end of the Zhou dynasty, the horses would all have
been used to pull conveyances rather than serving as mounts for equestrians.

2. See Waley's translation for his notes on this passage, p. 199 and p. 254. He
would disagree with my translation: "'*Chiao*' means here not the 'outskirts' of the
kingdom, but the mound on the outskirts of the capital, scene of the Great Sacrifice

(cf. Maspero, *La Chine Antique*, p. 225 seq.) which inaugurated the season's agriculture. To let weeds grow on this mound was a sacrilege; and to breed war horses upon it, a double profanation. For the Great Sacrifice is essentially connected with peace." He gives as evidence the end of the sixteenth chapter of the *Xun Zi*.

3. This text is present in the silk texts, the "*Jie Lao* 解老" and "*Yu Lao* 喻老" chapters of the *Han Fei Zi*, and in many other versions, but not in the Wang Bi text.

第四十七章

不出戶，知天下；
不窺牖，見天道。
其出彌遠，其知彌少。
是以聖人不行而知，
不見而〈名〉〔明¹〕，不爲而成。

47.

Know the whole world without going outdoors. Perceive the Dao of
Heaven without peeking out the window. The farther one goes the less one
knows. For this reason the Sage knows without going anywhere, perceives
clearly¹ without looking, and makes accomplishments without doing
anything.

NOTES:

1. The "*Jie Lao*" chapter of the *Han Fei Zi* and three variant texts all have *ming* 明
instead of *ming* 名. The ancient pronunciations (*miang* and *mieng*) differed only
slightly.

第四十八章

爲學日益，爲道日損。
損之又損，以至於無爲。
無爲而無不爲。
取天下常以無事，
及其有事，不足以取天下。

48.

One who engages in study is daily increased. One who engages in the Dao is daily diminished. Diminish and once again diminish until there is no activity. When there is no activity there is nothing that will not be done.[1] One always takes the world by means of not meddling. When one meddles then one is inadequate to take the world.

NOTES:

1. This chapter defines the idea of "non-action" as a limit case reached after successive approximations to perfect efficiency are made.

第四十九章

聖人無常心¹，以百姓心爲心。
善者吾善之，不善者吾亦善之，
德²善。
信者吾信之，不信者吾亦信之，
德信。
聖人在天下，歙歙焉；
爲天下渾其心。
百姓皆注其耳目，聖人皆孩之。

49.

The Sage has no constant mind.¹ He takes the minds of the common people to be his own.

Those who are good I treat as good. Those who are not good I also treat as good. Thereby I gain goodness.² The trustworthy I trust. The untrustworthy I also trust. Thereby I gain trust.

The Sage is closed off in respect to the world. For the sake of the world the Sage muddles his mind. The common people all strain their eyes and ears. [Yet] the Sage treats them all as little children.

NOTES:

1. Many versions, including the silk texts, invert the previous two characters.

2. This passage shows the practical identity of *de* 德 (virtue) and *de* 得 (acquire) in this entire text. Silk text B and thirteen others write *de* 得, and that character clearly reflects the intended meaning of this passage.

第五十章

出生入死。
生之徒十有三，死之徒十有三，
人之生，　動之死地亦十有三。
夫何故？以其生生之厚。
蓋聞善攝生者，陸行不遇兕虎，
入軍不被甲兵。
兕無所投其角，
虎無所措其爪，
兵無所容其双，
夫何故？以其無死地。

50.

Emerging is being born, entering is dying. Three out of ten are disciples of life. Three out of ten are disciples of death. Three out of ten move in the course of their lives toward the realm of death. For what reason? Because they would augment the richness of life.[1] Now I have heard that those who are good at aiding life when travelling on land do not encounter rhinoceroses and tigers. When they enter armed conflict they need not bear arms or armor. There is nowhere for the rhinoceros to gore with its horn. The tiger finds no place to sink its claws. Weapons find no place to lodge their blades. Why? Because there is no death-place in them.

NOTES:

1. Note the two other references to augmenting the richness of life, in chapters 55 and 75.

第五十一章

道生之，德畜之，
物形之，勢¹成之。
是以萬物莫不尊道而貴德。
道之尊，德之貴，
夫莫之命而常自然。
故道生之，〈德〉²畜之，長之，
育之，亭之，毒之，
養之，覆之³。
生而不有，爲而不恃⁴，
長而不宰。
是謂玄德。

51.

The Dao produces them. Virtue nurtures them. Creatures give them form. Power configurations[1] bring them to completion. For that reason none of the myriad creatures fails to respect the Dao and to revere virtue. No one orders this respect for the Dao and reverence of virtue, for it always occurs of its own accord. So the Dao produces them <and virtue>[2] cultivates them, fosters them, nurtures them, gives them refuge, gives them peace, rears them, and shelters them.[3] It produces them without seeking to possess them and acts without exacting gratitude.[4] It is senior to them yet does not rule over them. It is called the dark and mysterious virtue.

NOTES:

1. *Qi* 器 (utensil) is used in both silk texts instead of *shi* 勢 (power configuration). Compare this usage with the passage in chapter eleven about the empty space in the hub and in the shell of a house. The word I translate as "power configurations" is translated by Chan as "circumstances and tendencies" and by Wu as "environment."

2. Many texts, including the silk texts, omit this word. Without it the several activities (production, cultivation, etc.) fall into pairs.

3. The different versions of this line in the text are another indication to me that this book was passed down in an oral tradition and later written out by different scholars. Without more context than a mere list gives, it is difficult to tell for sure what each sound and meaning in the series should be. When unusual words appear, more ordinary alternatives to them appear in other versions of the text. The version given above is that of Wang Bi. The silk texts differ only in replacing *yu*育 (nurtures) with *sui* 遂 (Lau: accomplishes). This replacement suggests that *yu*育 may be a defective *sui* 隨 character. (*Sui* 遂 and *sui* 隨 have similar ancient pronunciations. See Karlgren, *Grammata Serica Recensa,* entries 11g and 526d.) But the next two verbs are both changed in the stone text. *Ting* 亭 and *du* 毒 (whose most common meanings are "pavilion" and "poison") are changed to *cheng* 成 and *shu* 熟 (which have the more easily understandable common meanings "bring to completion" and "ripen"). "*Ting*" has as its primary meaning "a building made to give safe refuge to travellers." (See Gao, p. 39.) And the *Guang-ya* dictionary says "*du*" means "peace." So these characters can have reasonable interpretations in the context of the above passage. It seems likely that the other characters occurred to some scholars, however.

4. The word *shi* 恃 is given various interpretations. Literally, it means "to depend on." Chan translates "rely on its own ability." Waley translates "lean on them." The real question is whether the Dao is said not to depend on its own act of doing, as Chan would have it, or whether it does not depend on the results of what it has done, i.e., it does not rest on its laurels. Possibly the original Chinese left the matter up in the air because it was intended to include both possibilities.

Commentary:

The last four sentences appear in chapter 10. The first two are also seen in chapter 2, and the last two are seen in chapter 77.

第五十二章

天下有始，以爲天下母。
既得其母，以知其子；
既知其子，復守其母，沒身不殆。
塞其兌，閉其門，終身不勤；
開其兌，濟其事，終身不救。
見小曰明，守柔曰强。
用其光，復歸其明，無遺身殃。
是爲〈習〉〔襲³〕常。

52.

The world has a beginning that acts as its mother. Once one attains to the mother, one can know the child. Having known the child, return to holding to the mother. Then one will be in no danger though one should lose one's body.[1] Plug your orifices, close your gates,[2] and you will be toil-free to the end of your life. If you open your orifices in order to aid in your endeavors, then you will never be rescued to the end of your days. To see the minute is called discernment. To hold to the pliant is called strength. To use your inner light to return once more to discernment and thus avoid abandoning yourself to danger is to depend on[3] the Constant.

NOTES:

1. Repeat of 16.

2. Repeat of 56.

3. This change is made in agreement with the silk texts.

第五十三章

使我介然有知，
行於大道，唯施是畏。
大道甚夷，而民好徑。
朝甚除，田甚蕪，倉甚虛；
服文綵，帶利劍，
厭飲食，財貨有餘，
是謂盜夸。
非道也哉！

53.

Should I have the least bit of knowledge, fear only that I might use it as I set out upon the great Dao. The great Dao is very smooth, yet people prefer the shortcuts. If the court is immaculate,[1] the fields will grow wild and the granaries will become very empty. To wear embroidered robes and strap on sharp swords, to satiate oneself with food and drink, and to have an excess of wealth and possessions [at such a time] is called banditry and excess. Oh! How such activities go against the Dao.

NOTES:

1. D. C. Lau (1963) translates *chu* 除 as "corrupt." I do not know the basis for his explanation of this character.

第五十四章

善建者不拔，善抱者不脱，
子孫以祭祀不輟。
修之於身，其德乃真；修之於家，
其德乃餘；
修之於鄉，其德乃長；修之於國，
其德乃豐；
修之於天下，其德乃普。
故以身觀身，以家觀家，
以鄉觀鄉，以國觀國，
以天下觀天下。
吾何以知天下然哉？以此。

54.

What is well built cannot be pulled up. What is well clasped cannot slip free.[1] By these means one's sons and grandsons will offer sacrifice unendingly. If it is cultivated in one's person, then virtue will be genuine. If it is cultivated in one's family, then virtue will be ample. If it is cultivated in one's local community, then virtue will be enduring. If it is cultivated in one's kingdom, then virtue will be plentiful. If it is cultivated in the world, then virtue will be universal. So observe each person in terms of that person himself, observe each family in terms of that family itself, observe each community in terms of that community itself. Observe each kingdom in terms of that kingdom itself. Observe the world in terms of the world itself. How do I know the way the world is? By this.

NOTES:

1. W. T. Chan interprets these two sentences to refer to one's adherence to the Dao.

第五十五章

含德之厚，比於赤子。
蜂蠆虺蛇[1]不螫，猛獸不據，
攫鳥不搏。
骨弱筋柔而握固，
未知牝牡之合而〔全〕〔朘[2]〕作，
精之至也。
終日號而不嗄，和之至也。
知和曰常，知常曰明。
益生曰祥。心使氣曰強。
物壯則老，謂之〈不〉〔否〕道。
〈不〉〔否[5]〕道早已。

55.

One possessing the fullness of virtue may be compared to a newborn baby. Hornets, scorpions, vipers, and snakes[1] cannot sting [the newborn baby]. The fierce beasts do not pounce upon it. The raptors do not sink their talons into it. The baby's bones are pliant, his muscles weak, yet his grip is firm. He has never known the coupling of male and female, yet has a full erection.[2] That is the height of vitality. He cries the entire day yet does not become hoarse. That is the perfection of harmony. To know harmony is said to be constant. To know constancy is said to be enlightenment. To augment life is said to be inauspicious.[3] For the heart and mind to exert compulsion on the lifebreath is said to be forcing things. When creatures come to their prime they begin to age. That[4] is spoken of as the dao (course) of retrograde action.[5] What is on the retrograde dao is soon finished.[6]

NOTES:

1. Very many other versions of the *Lao Zi* give "poisonous insects (*du chong* 毒蟲)" here, and it is argued on the basis of Wang's commentary that he had the same text. But the use of "poisonous insects" in his commentary could have been a paraphrase. The silk texts are very close to the Wang Bi version, so I have not changed the Wang Bi text at this point.

2. The silk texts have "penis of an infant (*juan* 朘) erects" instead of "completely (*quan* 全) erects" here.

3. Normally, the word given here means "auspicious." Note the prior passage on augmenting life, in chapter 50, and the passage ahead in chapter 75.

4. Any of the above choices which push the individual beyond the "infant" stage and is therefore to be avoided.

5. See Yan Ling-feng's *Lao Zi da-jie,* p. 125, and my note to the end of chapter 30.

6. See identical passage in chapter 30.

第五十六章

知者不言，言者不知。
塞其兌，閉其門，
挫其〈梲〉〔銳〕，
解其〈分〉〔紛²〕，
和其光，同其塵。
是謂玄同。
故不可得而親，不可得而疏；
不可得而利，不可得而害；
不可得而貴，不可得而賤。
故爲天下貴。

56.

Those who know do not talk. Those who talk do not know. [So:]
Stop up your orifices. Close your doors.[1] Blunt your sharpness. Release
your tangles.[2] Harmonize your lights. Make same your dust.[3] So doing is
called the dark and mysterious identity. Therefore [those who have
attained to the mysterious identity] cannot be made to be intimate, and they
cannot be alienated. They cannot be benefited, and they cannot be injured.
They cannot be ennobled, and they cannot suffer degradation. Therefore
they are noble among all those in the world.[4]

NOTES:

1. These two sentences occur also in chapter 52.

2. The Wang Bi text does not give the full form of this character.

3. This sentence also appears in chapter 4.

4. Chap. 62 also has these words.

第五十七章

以正治國，以奇用兵，
以無事取天下。
吾何以知其然哉？以此。
天下多忌諱，而民彌貧；
民多利器，國家滋昏；
人多伎巧，奇物滋起；
法令滋彰，盜賊多有。
故聖人云：
我無爲而民自化，
我好靜而民自正，
我無事而民自富，
我無欲而民自樸。

57.

Govern the kingdom with uprightness. Use weapons of war with guile. Take the world by means of non-doing. How do I know the way it is? By this: If there are many prohibitions in the world, then the people will become even poorer. If the people have many sharp weapons then the kingdom will become even more chaotic. If the people have many tricks then abnormal things will abound. If laws and commandments proliferate, then there will be large numbers of bandits and robbers. So the Sage says: I do nothing and the people transform of their own accord. I like tranquility and the people rectify themselves. I do not (have things to do =) meddle and the people themselves prosper. I have no desires and the people themselves come to the state of the Uncarved Block.

第五十八章

其政悶悶，其民惇惇；
其政察察，其民缺缺。
禍兮福之所倚，福兮禍之所伏。
孰知其極？其無正。
正復爲奇，善復爲妖。
人之迷，其日固久。
是以聖人方而不割，廉而不劌，
直而不肆，光而不耀。

58.

When governance is stifled, the people will be wholesome. When governance is exacting, the people will be shifty. Good fortune depends on disaster, and disaster [in turn] is concealed in good fortune. Who knows the end [of this cyclical process] or [the extent of] its irregularity? The straightforward changes into guile. Good changes into what is pernicious. This has indeed baffled people for a long time. For this reason the squares yet does not cut. He is probing[1] yet does no one injury. He is straight and yet does not force things into line. He is radiant and yet does not dazzle.

NOTES:

1. *Lian* 廉 has several meanings. Its most common meaning is "not avaricious." But it can also mean "an angle or corner" and thus give the idea of scrupulousness in some compounds. It also is used as a verb meaning "to investigate, to examine." See Mathews, entry 4003. Other authorities say it is used for *li* 利, sharp. All these meanings are also found in Gao, p. 410.

第五十九章

治人，事天，莫若嗇。
夫唯嗇，是謂早服；
早服謂之重積德；
重積德則無不克；
無不克則莫知其極；
莫知其極，可以有國；
有國之母，可以長久。
是謂深根固柢，長生久視之道。

59.

There is nothing as good as frugality for regulating the people and for serving Heaven. Now only frugality can be called an early compliance. An early compliance is spoken of as a double accumulation of virtue. When virtue is doubly accumulated, then there is nothing that is not overcome. When there is nothing that is not overcome, then no one can know your limit. When no one can know your limit, then you may possess the kingdom. When you have the mother of the kingdom, you can be long enduring. That is spoken of as the deep root, the firm-set trunk, the Way to long life and enduring vision.

第六十章

治大國，若烹小鮮。
以道蒞天下，其鬼不神（申）；
非其鬼不神（申），其神不傷人；
非其神不傷人，聖人亦不傷人。
夫兩不相傷，故德交歸焉。

60.

Regulating a large country is like boiling small fish. When the Dao is used to oversee the world, then its negative (contractive) forces of nature will not act as positive (expansive) forces.[1] Not [only] will its negative (contractive) forces not become positive (expansive) forces, [even] its spirits will not (pierce =) injure humans.[2] Not [only] will its spirits not injure humans, [even] extraordinarily talented humans will not injure people.[3] Now when these two do not injure each other, then virtuous interaction will return thereto.[4]

NOTES:

1. There being no extraneous activity, no side-effects are created in addition to the natural forces directly involved.

2. There being no side-effects, natural processes are not in any way injurious to humans. In their expansive movements they do not pierce and injure humans.

3. When the world of nature is entirely equable because the Dao has been used to oversee the world, the exceptional members of the human population will not be inclined to misbehave. Use of the Dao in overseeing the world has a direct effect on the exceptional humans, but also an indirect effect because its use has kept the

negative and positive forces of nature functioning normally so that they have no great adverse impact on humans.

4. I suspect that the previous line may have crept into the original text at some point in its history. In that case "these two" would refer to the positive and negative forces. As the text stands, "these two" would probably have to refer to the world and the extraordinarily talented human beings.

Commentary:

This is a very confusing chapter. The two silk texts offer no new direct suggestions for interpretation. The terms *gui* , *shen* and *sheng* are all in question. *Sheng* 聖 is normally translated as "the sage." But the dictionary definition is simply of one whose capacities are of the highest quality. The author may have had the Confucian sages in mind here. The terms *gui* 鬼 and *shen* 神 are usually understood as ghosts and spirits, but here they are apparently used to refer to natural forces rather than to supernatural entities. It seems that extraordinarily talented human beings are considered the most apt to harm people — probably because like all other human beings they have their subjective understandings of the world and their own self-centered motivations. Next most likely to harm people are "positive spirits" — probably the active forces of nature that can produce violent storms and other cataclysmic natural events. The least likely to harm people are "negative spirits," which must mean the things on the *yin* side of nature that are only inimical to humans to the extent that they *withdraw* what may be necessary for individual life or prosperity — the cooling of winter, the darkening of the sky at night, etc.

Most other translations interpret *gui* as "ghosts," but interpret *shen* as their *extension into the world* or active involvement with the world rather than as "spirits." Waley says in his Introduction to *The Way and Its Power*, p. 28, that "[*Shen*] comes from a root meaning 'to stretch,'" which is still the accepted explanation. (See Gao Shu-fan, pages 18 and 1172.) Waley's translation takes *shen* in two senses: (1) the "evil spirit" *gui* of a person in displaying its powers (i.e., extending into the world), and (2) the "good spirit" of a person.

Waley thinks the *gui* and *shen* mentioned both pertain to the ruler. Other interpreters of this passage take those two terms to have more general reference.

If one follows that general line of interpretation, then the passage must mean something like this:

When the Dao is used to oversee the world, its ghosts (negative spirits) do not display their powers. It is not that they do not display their powers, rather that the displaying of their powers does not harm people. It is not that the displaying of their powers does not harm people, but that the Sage as well does not harm people.

The first problem with this line of interpretation is that there is no good transition from the non-malignancy of the ghosts to the non-malignancy of the Sage.

The second problem with this line of interpretation is presented by the silk texts. In general, the form of the characters used to write the silk texts is under-determined. In the present case, the question in my mind is: Why did the scribes who wrote the silk texts not write 申 if they really meant "to extend?" They seem, to the contrary, to have felt the need to specify "spirits" by writing 神.

The *Lao Zi* is believed by some to have been composed before the time of Confucius. Others believe it to be a late Zhou dynasty product. Without getting into that argument here, we can say that one of the silk texts was written down at least as late as the late Zhou and the other silk text appears to be an early Han product.

If the time of transcription of the *Lao Zi* was at least as late as the end of the Zhou dynasty, then *yin-yang* ideas were already in wide currency. So it would not be impossible to find such ideas represented in this chapter regardless of whether they had occurred to the original author or authors of the *Lao Zi*.

Gui and *shen* form an *yin-yang* pair. The one is the negative image of the other.

The general theory presented in the Appendices to the *Book of Changes* is that members of *yin-yang* pairs may spontaneously transform, the one into the other. So *gui* may transform into *shen* and vice-versa. Or at least there is the potential for such a transformation under appropriate circumstances.

If a *gui* should begin to "display its powers" or "extend" (*shen* 申), that is, if what was previously *yin* and absorptive, quiet, and treasuring away in its mode of operation should become *yang* or active and intrusive in its operation, then it would become a "spirit" (*shen* 神) by virtue of its new ontological status.

For what is normally a "negative" part of nature, such as the cold of winter, to become "positive" in action like the heat of summer would be anomalous, unless it occurred in the ordinary way of transition from *yin* to *yang* such as occurs when winter gives way to spring and then to summer. Merely by being anomalous such a development might bring harm to human beings.

But there are also naturally *yang* phenomena in nature which may sometimes fail to be in harmony with the needs of human beings. By nature active and perhaps intrusive, these forces may easily do damage to human beings, as when violent storms create catastrophes.

Finally, on another level, there are human beings, and the most talented of them also have the potential to do the most damage if their actions are not in harmony with the needs of the general population.

It seems to me that this chapter may reflect the general division of the universe into the domains of earth, heaven, and human beings.

So I think that the most satisfactory explanation for this chapter is to say that it talks about the need for harmony and tranquility in three domains: the domain of the *yin* forces, called *gui,* the domain of the *yang* forces, called *shen,* and the domain of the human activities of which the most far-reaching in effect are those of the *sheng ren* — those exceptional human beings that we often call sages.

This chapter asserts that when the Dao is used to oversee the world, the forces in the *yin* domain will not spill over into the proper domain of the *yang* to create problems, the forces in the *yang* domain will likewise not create disasters by acting in great turmoil, and, finally, the most problematical forces in the human world will not go awry.

·Therefore I take the first and second characters pronounced *shen* (here written 神) to be a mistake for its cognate written 中. But I believe that the third and fourth *shen* characters are properly written 神 and refer to positive spirits (and not merely to the "extensions" of the negative spirits in various activities).

Mention of *gui* (negative spirits, spirits that have been "gathered in," "ghosts") and *shen* (positive spirits, spirits that "extend") provides a natural bridge to mention of the *sheng ren* (exceptional human beings or "sages").

For the foregoing reasons my translation of this chapter differs considerably from that of most interpreters of the *Lao Zi*.

第六十一章

大國者下流，
天下之〈交〉〔牝¹〕。
天下之〈牝〉〔交¹〕，
牝常以靜勝牡，以靜爲下。
｛故宜爲下也。²｝
故大國以下小國，則取小國；
小國以下大國，
則取〔於³〕大國。
故或下以取，或下而取。
大國不過欲兼畜人，
小國不過欲入事人。
夫兩者各得其所欲，大者宜爲下。

61.

A large country is at the low end of the watershed. It takes the role of the female[1] in the world. In the interactions that take place in the world, the female always overcomes the male by means of her tranquility. Because of her tranquility the female is the lower one. (Therefore it is appropriate that she be lower.)[2] So if the large country takes the lower position with regard to the smaller countries, it can then take the smaller countries. If the smaller countries take the lower position with regard to the larger country, then they can {be} take{n by}[3] the larger country. So either one is lower in order to take, or lower in order to be taken. The larger country only desires to foster all of the people. The smaller countries only desire to enter into the service of others. Now when the two sides each have gotten what they desire, it is appropriate that the larger country still take the lower role.

NOTES:

1. Both the silk texts show these two words interchanged. The reading in the silk texts makes the sense of this chapter much clearer.

2. This sentence occurs in both the silk texts.

3. The two silk texts have *yu* 於 at this point, which makes the sense of the passage clearer.

第六十二章

道者萬物之奧¹。
善人之寶，不善人之所保。
人之不善，何棄之有？²
美言可以市〔人〕∠³尊行可以
〈加〉〔賀⁴〕人。
故立天子，置三公，
雖有拱璧以先駟馬，
不如坐進此道。
古之所以貴此道者何？不曰：
《〈以〉〔不⁵〕求〔以⁶〕得，
有罪以免》邪？
故為天下貴。

62.

The Dao is sanctum for the myriad creatures.¹ It is the treasure of the good person, and what protects the person who is not good. How can people who are not good be abandoned?² Beautiful words can be marketed [to people].³ Fine behavior can be presented to people.⁴ So in enthroning a Son of Heaven or in installing one of the three great ministers, reverently offering a jade ceremonial disk as a preliminary to presenting a chariot and team of four is not as good as kneeling to offer this Dao. Why was this Dao esteemed in antiquity? Is it not said: "By it one attains with{out?}⁵ seeking.⁶ By it one escapes from one's transgressions?" Therefore it is prized by the world.

NOTES:

1. In the first line, the silk texts have "*zhu* 注" (to pour, to inject, etc.) instead of "*ao* 奧." Chan says of "*ao*" that it is "the southwestern corner of the house, the most highly honored place in the house, where family worship was carried out, grains and treasures were stored, etc." The character given in the silk texts does not make sense to me here, but another, "*zhu* 主" originally depicted the burning wick of a lamp and thus suggests the idea of "the center of attention," or perhaps even an altar lamp.

2. This line and the following two lines have been exchanged. The parts of this chapter that are about good people belong together, and so do the parts about offering words of advice or models for behavior.

3. Something is probably wrong with this line. As it stands, it either says: "Beautiful words can (market=) gain respect. Behavior can cause people to count one as important," or it says: "Beautiful words can be marketed. Respectable behavior can cause people to count one as important. The *Huai-nan Zi* has 美言可以市尊，美行可以加人。 "Beautiful words can gain respect. Beautiful behavior can cause people to count one as important." But the A silk text punctuates (∠) after *shi* and A and B have *he* 賀 (bestow) for *jia* 加. Beautiful words can be marketed. Fine behavior can be presented to people." I am more happy with the silk text version since the explanations of *jia* in this passage have always seemed strained to me. But the *Huai-nan Zi* and various modern texts seem to feel the need for an indirect object for "to market" so I have supplied *ren*.

4. This emendation is according to the silk texts, as explained in note 3.

5. The text is probably scrambled again in the last two lines. I have added a second negative, *bu*, in curly brackets. No texts known to me actually have this character, but it is easy to see how a character could have dropped out at this point that so closely follows another *bu*. Furthermore, adding a fourth character to this phrase makes a better parallel construction with the following phrase. (Yan Ling-feng thinks the original *bu* and *yue* have been inverted. See his *Lao Zi da-jie*, p. 257.)

6. I rearrange the Wang Bi text at this point to agree with many other versions (including the B silk text), and to make this and the following phrase more nearly parallel in structure. But the sentence is still strange, since under a more strict interpretation the last phrase says: "By means of having transgressions one escapes." That does not seem to be what the original author intended to convey, but to fix the sentence would require a more substantial modification than seems warranted.

第六十三章

為無為，事無事，味無味。
大小多少，報怨以德。
圖難於其易，為大於其細。
天下難事，必作於易；
天下大事，必作於細。
是以聖人終不為大，故能成其大。
夫輕諾必寡信，多易必多難。
是以聖人猶難之，故終無難矣。

63.

Act by nonaction. Do by not doing. Find flavor in blandness. Magnify the small. Augment the few. Respond to enmity with virtue. Solve difficult problems while they are still easy. Do great tasks while they are yet small. The difficult problems of the world must be solved while they are still easy. The great tasks of the world must be done while they are still small.[1] For this reason the Sage never undertakes great projects, and so he can accomplish great things.[2] When acquiescence is given lightly, trust must be diminished. When things are oversimplified, difficulty must be magnified. So the Sage treats things as even more difficult [than they would seem to be], and [so] in the end there is no difficulty.

NOTES:

1. It is also possible to interpret these two lines to mean: "The difficult problems of the world must arise from what is easy. The great tasks of the world must arise from what is small." However, that interpretation leaves these two sentences unconnected to the sentence that follows them.

2. Repeated from chapter 34.

第六十四章

其安易持，其未兆易謀，
其脆易〈泮〉〔判[1]〕，其微易散。
為之於未有，治之於未亂。
合抱之木，生於毫末；
九層之臺，起於累土；
千里之行，始於足下。
為者敗之，執者失之。
是以聖人無為，故無敗，
無執，故無失。
民之從事，常於幾成而敗之。
慎終如始，則無敗事。
是以聖人欲不欲，不貴難得之貨；
學不學，復眾人之所過。
以輔萬物之自然，而不敢為。

64.

It is easy to maintain control of things while they are still quiescent. It is easy to plan for them before they have given any inkling. When things are crisp, they are easy to shear off.[1] When things are minute, they are easily dispersed. Do it before they come into existence! Regulate them before they become disordered! A tree of two spans starts as the finest filament. A tower of nine stories begins by heaping up dirt. A journey of a thousand miles begins beneath one's feet. Those who do things defeat [their goals].

Those who clutch at things lose them.[2] For that reason the Sage has no activity and so suffers no defeats. He clutches at nothing and so loses nothing. In pursuing their objectives the people constantly fail when they are about to succeed. If you are as careful of conclusions as you are of beginnings,[3] then you will not ruin things. For that reason the Sage desires not to desire,[4] and does not value scarce commodities. He learns non-learning, in order to return to what the multitudes have passed by, and thereby can aid in the natural processes of the myriad creatures without daring to act forcefully.

NOTES:

1. I follow Waley in, "reading *p'an* with the 'knife' determinative," and write 判.

2. This sentence also appears in chapter 29.

3. A similar sentiment is expressed in the *Zuo Zhuan* 左傳, Duke Xiang 襄, the twenty-fifth year. In his note to this passage, Waley says: "For similar sayings see *Book of History*, Legge, pp. 183 and 211."

4. If the sage can maintain a desireless state, then he can perceive the *miao*, the inexplicable efficacies, the marvels of creation, and so know how the world really works. See my commentary to the first chapter and the appendices.

第六十五章

古之善爲道者，
非以明民，將以愚之。
民之難治，以其智多。
故以智治國，國之賊；
不以智治國，國之福。
知此兩者亦〈稽〉〔楷[1]〕式。
常知〈稽〉〔楷〕式，是謂玄德。
玄德深矣，遠矣，與物反矣！
然後乃至大順。

65.

Those of antiquity who were good at the practice of the Dao did not enlighten people — rather, they made them ignorant. The people are difficult to regulate when they are too clever. So to use cleverness to regulate a country is to do injury to the country. To not use cleverness to regulate a country is to be a benefactor to the country. Knowing these two alternatives constitutes a model. Having a constant awareness of this model is called the dark and mysterious virtue. The dark and mysterious virtue is profound and remote. It is opposed to [the ordinary inclinations of] creatures and so comes into a great confluence [with the total process of the universe].[2]

NOTES:

1. The first character, *ji*, means "together, same," whereas the second character, *jie*, means "model, pattern." It appears that a near homonym was written for the correct character in the Wang Bi text.

2. Alternate interpretation: It gives creatures their return (to innocence), and so they afterwards come into a great compliance with the Dao.

第六十六章

江海所以能爲百谷王者，
以其善下之，故能爲百谷王。
是以欲上民，必以言下之；
欲先民，必以身後之。
是以聖人處上而民不重；
處前而民不害。
是以天下樂推而不厭。
以其不爭，故天下莫能與之爭。

66.

The reason that the great rivers and the seas can be the kings of the
hundred valleys is that they are good at lying beneath them. Thus they can
be the kings of the hundred valleys. So if one would be superior to people,
one must by words put oneself beneath them. If one would lead the people,
one must put one's person (i.e., interests) behind them. For that reason,
although the Sage is on top, the people do not perceive him to be a burden.
Although he is in front of them, the people do not take that to be an
injury. So the world takes joy in pushing him to the fore and does not
become tired of him. Because he does not contend, no one in the world
can contend with him.

第六十七章

天下皆謂我道大，似不肖。
夫唯大，故似不肖。
若肖，久矣其細也夫。
我有三寶，持而保之。
一曰慈，二曰儉，
三曰不敢爲天下先。
慈故能勇，儉故能廣，
不敢爲天下先，故能成器長。
今舍慈且勇，舍儉且廣，
舍後且先，死矣！
夫慈，以戰則勝，以守則固。
天將救之，以慈衛之。

67.

Everyone in the world says that my Dao is great and yet it does not seem so. Now only because it is great does it not seem so. If it seemed so, then long would it have been petty. I have three treasures that I uphold and protect: The first is called compassion, the second is called thrift, the third is not being willing to be first in the world. Being compassionate, one is able to be brave. Being thrifty, one is able to be generous. Not being willing to be first in the world, one is able to become the Chief Agent [of the processes of the universe that constitute the manifestations of the Dao]. Now should one abandon compassion and yet seek to act bravely, should one abandon thrift and yet seek to be generous, or abandon one's position at the rear and yet seek to be foremost, then it will be fatal. And if one wages war with compassion then one will win. If one seeks to defend something by using compassion then it will be secure. What Heaven will give salvation, it protects by means of compassion.

第六十八章

善爲士者不武，善戰者不怒，
善勝敵者不與，善用人者爲之下。
是謂不爭之德，是謂用人之力，
是謂配天〈古[1]〉之極。

68.

Those who are good at being knights are not martial. Those who are good at warfare do not rage. Those who are good at overcoming their adversaries do not join issue. Those who are good at employing others put themselves beneath them. That is called the virtue of non-contention. That is called the power to employ others. That is called the perfection attained by becoming a match with Heaven.[1]

NOTES:

1. The character *gu* appearing at this point seems to be extraneous, but the silk texts both have it and only one of them has a character apparently meant to be pei 配, which is *fei* 肥 or 妃. (Oddly, D. C. Lau omits this character in his version of the silk texts.) Since the silk texts do not have *zhi li* 之力, Henricks translates: "This is called [correctly] using men; / This is called matching Heaven./ It's the high point of the past." He observes that they form parallel sentences that rhyme. The Wang Bi text, with *gu* deleted, also forms parallel sentences, and the last three lines rhyme. Nevertheless, it seems likely that Henricks is correct. First an early redactor added *zhi li* to parallel the *zhi de* in 不爭之德. That made *pei tian* 配 — and *gu zhi ji* 古之極 both seem too short.

Commentary:

One is a match with Heaven in the sense that one is totally impartial and not in any sense driven by subjective views.

第六十九章

用兵有言：
《吾不敢爲主而爲客，
不敢進寸而退尺。》
是謂行無〈行〉〔形¹〕，攘²無臂，
扔³無敵，執無兵。
禍莫大於輕敵，輕敵幾喪吾寶。
故抗兵相〈加〉〔若⁵〕，
哀者勝矣。

69.

There is a saying about using armed forces: "I dare not be the host (i.e., the initiator) and instead become the guest. I dare not advance an inch, but rather retreat a foot." That is called to make troop movements without form,[1] shoving aside[2] without a forearm, destroying[3] without involving an enemy, and wielding arms without there being a weapon. There is no greater disaster than underestimating one's enemy. If one were to underestimate one's enemy that would be tantamount to losing one's treasures.[4] So when troops of equivalent strength[5] are opposed, the side that goes into battle with sorrow will win.[6]

NOTES:

1. The first xing 行 refers to military movements, troop movements. The second xing 行 is a mistake for xing 形 meaning visible form. See Yan Ling-feng, *Lao Zi Da Jie*, 284.

2. *Rang* 攘 means *tui* 推 (to push) according to *Shuo-wen Jie-zi* 説文解字. See Yan, *loc. cit.*

3. *Reng* 扔 means *cui* 摧 (to destroy). See Yan, *loc. cit.*

4. Presumably the three treasures mentioned in chapter 67.

5. The silk texts have *ruo* 若 instead of *jia* 加. Other texts also have *ruo*.

6. Compare to the passage about generals of the left and right, chapter 31.

第七十章

吾言甚易智，甚易行。
天下莫能知，莫能行。
言有宗，事有君。
夫唯無知，是以不我知。
知我者希，則我〈者〉貴。[1]
是以聖人被褐懷玉。

70.

My words are extremely easy to know and extremely easy to put into practice. No one in the world is able to know them or to put them into operation. [My] sayings have ancestors, and events have rulers. Now only because they do not know them do they not (know =) understand me. Those who know me are few, and so I am precious.[1] For that reason the Sage cloaks himself with a rough garment and holds his jade to his bosom.

NOTES:

1. The silk texts and twenty-five others all say "*ze wo gui* " (so I am precious) instead of "*ze wo zhe gui* " (those who emulate me are precious) which makes a better connection with the last sentence of this chapter.

第七十一章

知不知，上。
不知〔不¹〕知，病。
夫唯病病，是以不病。²
聖人不病，以其病病，是以不病。

71.

To know that you do not know is the best. To not know that you {do not} know is a defect.¹ Now only by treating defect as defect can you be without defect.² The Sage is without defect because he treats [all] defects as defects and so is without defect.³

NOTES:

1. Yan Ling-feng suggested this emendation without adducing any textual evidence. Now the silk texts show that he was probably correct. In the A silk text this line was written 不 = 知 = . It is easy to imagine that one of the Chinese ditto marks might have been inadvertently ignored at some point in the transmission of the text thus producing the version found in all other extant texts.

2. The third sentence is missing from both silk texts. It could have crept in from an early commentary.

3. Compare this chapter to the *Analects of Confucius*, 2:17.

第七十二章

民不畏威，則大威至。
無〈狎〉〔狹¹〕其所居，無〈厭〉
〔壓²〕其所生。
夫唯不〈厭〉〔壓〕，是以不〈厭〉
〔壓〕。
是以聖人自知不自見，
自愛不自貴。
故去彼取此。

72.

When the people do not fear terrible things, then the great terrors arrive. [Therefore:] Do not restrict the range of their daily activities. Do not oppress them in their livelihood. Now it is only by not oppressing them that they will not find your presence oppressive. For this reason the Sage knows himself but does not show himself. He loves himself but does not exalt himself. So he rids himself of that and accepts this.[3]

NOTES:

1. This alteration is made in agreement with the stone text and many other versions. Chan says the original character also means "narrow." The silk texts use two rare characters, both of which have the same phonetic element as does Wang Bi's character.

2. *Yan* ("satiated") has been mistakenly written for *ya* ("to press down").

3. Chap. 12 and chap. 38 also have this line.

第七十三章

勇於敢則殺，勇於不敢則活。
此兩者，或利或害，
天之所惡，孰知其故？
〈是以聖人猶難之。¹〉
天之道，不爭而善勝，
不言而善應，不召而自來，
〈繟〉〔坦²〕然而善謀。
天網恢恢，疏而不失。

73.

When one is brave at acting bold then one will be killed. When one is brave at not acting bold then one will live. [Of] these two [one] may involve benefit [and one may involve] injury. Who knows the reason for what Heaven hates? <For that reason the Sage treats it as especially difficult.¹ > The Dao of Heaven does not contend and yet is good at winning, does not speak and yet is good at responding, does not summon yet things come to it of their own accord, is in repose and yet good at laying plans. The vast net of Heaven is coarse, yet nothing escapes it.

NOTES:

1. Repeated from 63 by mistake. Not present in the Dun-huang or silk texts.

2. See Jiang, p. 431.

第七十四章

民不畏死，奈何以死懼之？
若使民常畏死，而爲奇者，
吾得執而殺之，孰敢？
常有司殺者殺。夫代司殺者殺，
是謂代大匠斲。夫代大匠斲者，
希有不傷其手矣。

74.

If the people do not fear death, how can anyone use [the threat of] death to intimidate them? Supposing the people to be caused to be constantly in fear of death and at the same time to regard it as an unusual event — should I [be prepared to] seize and have them killed, then who would dare [perform the execution]?[1] There is always an executioner to do the killing. To take the place of the executioner to kill is said to be [like] taking the place of the great lumberman to chop wood. Now one who takes the place of the great lumberman to chop wood seldom avoids injuring his own hand.[2]

NOTES:

1. Most commentators and translators have chosen to follow Wang Bi and others in interpreting this sentence in a different way: "If the people be caused to always fear death, and yet [some of them] behave in deviant ways, then should I seize and kill them, who would dare act that way?" As Jiang Xi-chang points out, under this interpretation, the "I" in this sentence must then refer to the executioner mentioned below, or else the author would appear to contradict himself. It seems very odd to me to have the speaker in this chapter suddenly take on the identity of nature itself — which is surely what the great executioner must be.

2. The superficial interpretation of this passage, which may lead rulers to use a general policy of forbearance punctuated by random killings of extraordinary brutality, is that if death is not such an ever-present threat that people feel it better to be killed for a wolf than for a sheep, then the occasional execution will instill terror in a meek populace. Besides reeking of the manipulative use of terror by authoritarian regimes, that interpretation has the disadvantage that it leaves the remainder of the chapter unconnected to anything that was earlier said. My interpretation suggests that it is the Dao that kills rightly, and anyone else who presumes to do so risks violence rebounding on his own person.

第七十五章

民之饑，以其上食稅之多，
是以饑。
民之難治，以其上之有爲，
是以難治。
民之輕死，以其上求生之厚，
是以輕死。
夫唯無以生爲者，是賢於貴生。

75.

The reason that the people starve is that their superiors consume so much tax grain. For this reason do they starve. The reason the people are difficult to govern is that their superiors are officious. For this reason are they difficult to govern. The reason the people view death lightly is that their superiors seek to augment the richness of life.[1] For this reason do they view death lightly. Now only those who do not do things to augment life are good at valuing life.

NOTES:

1. Compare the passages on augmenting the richness of life in chapters 50 and 55.

第七十六章

人之生也柔弱，其死也堅強。
萬物草木之生也柔脆，
其死也枯槁。
故堅強者死之徒，柔弱者生之徒。
是以兵強則不勝，
木強則〈兵〉〔柜²〕。
強大處下，柔弱處上。

76.

In life people are soft and supple. In death they are hard and rigid. Among the myriad creatures, the grasses and trees in life are pliant and crisp, but in death they are brittle and withered. So the hard and rigid are the disciples of death, and the soft and supple are the disciples of life.[1] For that reason, when armies are powerful they will not win. When trees are rigid they will be terminated.[2] The rigid and large take the lower position while the soft and supple take the upper position.

NOTES:

1. See "disciples of life," chapter 50. The word I have translated "rigid" in this chapter is normally translated as "strong."

2. Various characters appear at this point in various editions. The characters that appear in the silk texts make less sense than some of the others. None, however, seems to really fit the context. It almost seems that when people came to write this book down nobody knew what character to write here. D. C. Lau transforms the character *heng* 恆 in the A silk text into *geng* 柜 by adding a wood radical 木 to

the left side. That character is not a common one, but it appears to refer to the natural termination of the life of a tree. *Geng* rhymes with *sheng* in the line above. Incidentally, there are two other characters based on *heng* used in the silk texts, but those two characters are not found in modern dictionaries.

第七十七章

天之道，其猶張弓與！
高者抑之，下者舉之；
有餘者損之，不足者補之。
天之道，損有餘而補不足；
人之道，則不然，
損不足以奉有餘。
孰能有餘以奉天下？唯有道者。
是以聖人為而不恃，功成而不處，
其不欲見賢。

77.

The Dao of Heaven (i.e., the process of the universe) is like the drawing of a bow — the high end [of the bow] is pulled down and the low end is pulled up. What has an excess is depleted and what is inadequate is augmented. The Dao of Heaven works to deplete whatever has an excess and to augment whatever is inadequate. The dao of human beings is not this way. It depletes what is already inadequate to present to what already has an excess.[1] Who can have a surplus to present to the world? Only those who have the Dao. For that reason the Sage acts without exacting gratitude.[2] When his accomplishments are made he does not dwell on them,[3] such is his unwillingness to manifest his worthiness.

NOTES:

1. See the passage on holding the debtor's portion of the tally, chapter 79.

2. Same sentence in chapters 2, 10, 51.

3. Compare chapter 2.

第七十八章

天下莫柔弱於水，
而攻堅強者莫之能勝。
以其無以易之。
弱之勝強，柔之勝剛，
天下莫不知，莫能行。
是以聖人云：
《受國之垢，是謂社稷主；
受國不祥，是謂天下王。》
正言若反。

78.

There is nothing in the world more soft and supple than water. But nothing can surpass it for attacking the hard and rigid because there is nothing by which they can change it. None in the world fail to know that the supple overcomes the rigid and that the soft overcomes the hard, but none can put this knowledge into practice. For that reason the Sage says: He who receives the dirt of the kingdom is called the master of the shrine to Earth and Millet.[1] He who takes up the inauspicious affairs of the kingdom is called the king of the world. Correct sayings seem to have things turned upside-down.

NOTES:

1. According to the prescribed rituals of the Zhou dynasty, when a man was enfeoffed as a lord of a feudal domain, he was given a clod of earth from the part of the shrine to the earth that corresponded to his part of the Zhou territory. But the king of the Zhou must have had original possession of all of the earth in that altar. So in some sense he must have received the dirt of the entire kingdom when he ascended to the throne, even though there was no need to physically transport any soil. In this passage Lao Zi calls attention to the metaphorical meaning of this "receiving of the dirt of the kingdom" — it should not be regarded as an odious thing.

第七十九章

和大怨，必有餘怨，安可以爲善？
是以聖人執左契，而不責於人。
有德司契，無德司徹。
天道無親，常與善人。

79.

After harmonizing a great grievance there must remain a residue of enmity. How can that be regarded as good? For that reason the Sage takes the left portion of the contract tally[1] rather than trying to make (contractual) demands on people. Those who have virtue take charge of [fulfilling obligations of] the contract. Those who have no virtue take charge of exaction. The Dao of Heaven has no one to whom it is close by birth. It always gives to the good person.[2]

NOTES:

1. Wing-tsit Chan, Carus, Waley, Blakney, Lin Yutang, and Henricks say that the left-hand portion of a contract tally was given to the debtor. D. C. Lau, p. 115, says the left-hand portion is the creditor's portion. The *Zhong Wen Da Ci Dian* does not say which part of the tally the debtor gets, but in the definition of "left" it gives eight meanings out of ten which indicate that being on the left connoted inferior status or condition. The one instance in which left has a good connotation is the case of mourning practice, which we have already seen in chapter 31. See Henricks's note, p. 184, for more opinions.

2. See Arthur Waley's excellent discussion of this passage.

第八十章

小國寡民，使有什伯之器而不用，
使民重死而不遠徙。
雖有舟輿，無所乘之；
雖有甲兵，無所陳之。
使〈人〉〔民²〕復結繩而用之。
甘其食，美其服，
安其居，樂其俗。
鄰國相望，雞犬之聲相聞，
民至老死不相往來。

80.

Diminish the size and population of a country. Let them have the utensils
of squads and platoons yet be unwilling to use them. Let the people take
death as a serious matter and so not venture far away, and even though
they have boats and carts, not ride in them. Even though they have shields
and edged weapons, let them not ever display them.[1] Let the people revert
to recording information by knotting cords. Let them relish their food,
find their clothing beautiful, be content with their dwellings, and take joy
in their customs. Although they be within sight of neighboring kingdoms,
so that they can hear each others' dogs and roosters, let them never visit
back and forth all the days of their lives.

NOTES:

1. Earlier (chapter 36) Lao Zi mentioned that weapons were like fish in that they could not be safely removed from their nurturing medium. Again, in this chapter, we see that he advises against displaying them. They are to be kept in their sheaths and stored in armories, not flaunted about.

2. See Jiang, p. 463.

第八十一章

信言不美，美言不信。
善者不辯，辯者不善。
知者不博，博者不知。
聖人不積，
既以爲人己愈有，
既以與人己愈多。
天之道，利而不害；
聖人之道，爲而不爭。

81.

Trustworthy words are not fine-sounding, and fine-sounding words are not trustworthy. Good people do not engage in disputation, and those who engage in disputation are not good people. Those who are wise are not erudite, and those who are erudite are not wise. The Sage does not accumulate things. Since what he does is for the people he has more than enough for himself. Since he gives things to the people he has even more himself. The Dao of Heaven benefits and does not injure. The Dao of the Sage does things and does not contend.

INTRODUCTION
TO THE
GREAT LEARNING (Da Xue)
AND THE
DOCTRINE OF THE MEAN (Zhong Yong)

Reasons to be interested in the *Great Learning* and the *Doctrine of the Mean*

The Confucian tradition excelled in attracting dedicated people to service

Over the centuries since the founding of the Zhou dynasty, which according to tradition occurred in 1122 B.C., succeeding dynasties and regimes have recruited intelligent men of high character to a vision of service to their nation and to their fellow human beings. While there have undeniably been those who sought selfish gain or personal power, and have in other ways failed the ideals put forth in Confucian thought, there have also been examples of the highest altruism in service to the general polity and of the greatest courage in opposing what these people saw to be bad policies or bad behavior on the part of government officials or even on the part of the rulers.

Offers a counterbalance to coercive approaches

Although China went through a period of extreme totalitarian rule during the Qin dynasty (221–207 B.C.) and has recently experienced another period of dictatorial rule, in general the Chinese polity was protected from disorder without blatant dependence on the repression of social or political opposition. In most cases, people were attracted to service not only because a position in government brought status and material rewards, but also because of a genuine idealism and desire to serve. So it seems clear to me that Chinese society has a generally effective way of securing the firm allegiance of almost all of its members, and that the method used does not depend on extrinsic motivating factors such as high salaries or fear of punishment.

Facilitate, enlist, engage, recruit, *educare*, "turn on to?"

I find that I lack the proper English word to convey in a positive sense what the cultural inventions used by Chinese society have been able to do to secure the cooperation of talented people in the service of government. The social interaction of which I speak is an action performed by established members of the community upon potential members of that same community. However, it is not in any sense a compulsion visited upon them. By means of this activity, the teachers and other leaders of society empower the youth of that society to become fully functional human beings, to become fully integrated members of the society who wholeheartedly give their cooperation and energies to it and therefore acquire the power to influence their environment in ways that are beneficial to all. They enlist the energies of these young people in an ongoing social project that is intended to benefit and is perceived as benefiting the members of the society. They engage the minds, the wills, and the energies of these young people in the duties of the stewardship of the entire community. They recruit them into a community that is not ruled by fear or driven by greed. And since it appears that we do not even have an English word for this activity, it is possible that we neglect its performance in our own society. Perhaps we accomplish it only by accident or as the by-product of trying to do something else. And perhaps this is why our society experiences more and more problems.

The nearest I can now come to naming this activity in English is to call it "unblindfolding." Let me try to explain what I mean by that term. Suppose that there were some activity of value that someone had never tried, and the reason that he had never tried it was that his vision of it was obscured, or he was prevented in some other way from becoming aware of the activity. Because he was unaware of it, he could never try it and therefore could never learn to love the satisfaction that it brings. It would then be a service to that person to remove the blindfold from his eyes, to open the channels of his perception, so that he might find out for himself how worthy and satisfying the activity actually is.

Let us take a homely example, the eating of some form of good and delicious food. Someone might never have perceived some foodstuff as a possible source of nourishment, perhaps because its appearance resembled that of a poisonous substance, or perhaps because of some other impediment or prejudice that stood in the way of that person's trying the substance as a possible food. In such a case, all that might be necessary to make it become a regular part of that person's diet would be for somebody else to alert him or her to the possibility of eating it. Once having sampled the new foodstuff, the person in question could be depended upon to continue using it because of its good taste and general benefits to health.

One of the strongest points of traditional Chinese society is that it opens the individual to the perception that society is a beneficial institution for human beings, and that work done in the service of the society is satisfying to the individual who performs that work.

This Chinese view of society and of work done in its service is, in origin, a religious perception. The earliest leaders of the Zhou dynasty (*c.* 1027–256 B.C.) taught that the world is the domain of a good god who aims for the well-being of all humans and puts humans to the task of stewardship so that the world can be preserved as a suitable environment in which they can live. Originally, the Zhou political leaders taught that the Zhou king had the right to rule because Heaven had selected him to rule on account of his moral excellence. But they also taught that this mandate to rule, which he and his royal house had received, might be withdrawn at any time for failure to do the will of Heaven. So the duty was incumbent upon them to learn about and to understand the will of Heaven, and to carry out its requirements.

By the time of Confucius, that idea had been broadened so that it was considered to be the general responsibility of everyone to do the will of Heaven. However, there was no idea that divine sanctions would be imposed upon anyone who failed to do so. Then how did the Chinese succeed in attracting the allegiance of so many fine and talented people to the service of this ideal?

What seems to me to have happened is that throughout history since the early Zhou dynasty the leaders of the Chinese moral community have succeeded in opening the minds of their young people to the vision of a worthy cause in whose service they willingly devote their energies. Rather than threatening people with punishment if they did not obey the Zhou's regulations, the Zhou leaders asked each person, in effect, whether he or she could be satisfied to be less as a person than he or she really could be. Knowing, they asked, that there is an immensely worthy project and plan for the world in which you might take part, and knowing that participating in the work of that plan can be immensely satisfying for many kinds of reasons, can you be satisfied to sit on the sidelines and indulge yourself in seeking some lesser pleasures?

Neither Confucius nor Mencius was a moralizer. Neither of these men sought to impose his will on other people by direct threats or threats of divine sanction (save that they did subscribe to the theory that Heaven would remove its divine mandate to rule from the current royal house if the rulers failed to work for the benefit of the people). They created a philosophy and an ethos that has been a major component of the Chinese way of life ever since. The teachers who have continued in their tradition have successfully passed down the vision originally opened up to them by the earlier statesmen and philosophers of the Zhou dynasty.

Neither Confucius nor Mencius indoctrinated his students. To them, to do so would be as misguided as to try to indoctrinate a child to like ice cream. They did not use fear, hatred, or any of the other base emotions to ring their followers in. However, it appears that not all of those who spoke as the moral leaders of the Zhou practiced such useful restraint. The activities of the moralizers among the early Confucians led by way of a critical reaction to the development of Daoist philosophy, which in turn led to changes in Confucianism.

World-View of the *Lao Zi*

"Anti-Establishment" reaction against Confucian orthodoxy

By reading the *Lao Zi*, the reader can learn that there must have been many people after the time of Confucius who spoke in the name of orthodox Zhou dynasty religious and philosophical belief and, rather than opening people up to the vision of the ideal society that they could help provide for themselves, simply specified the desired final behavior and demanded that behavior of people. So Lao Zi indicates that, just as Confucius had warned in a general way, when the external manifestations of benevolence and filial piety were demanded of people, then they reacted to this coercion by producing only the semblance of benevolence and filial piety. When true benevolence became a sham, the establishment leaders demanded *yi*, which means both "justice" and "a sense of right and wrong." The people again responded by creating the appearance of seeking justice and responding to a sense of right and wrong. The second virtue having become a sham, the leaders demanded a lower and more superficial virtue, a "sense of propriety." When finally that virtue proved hollow as well, the moralizers turned to the raw use of force to compel the results that they wanted.

Daoism is Shamanic in Religious Background

In my opinion, the Daoist philosophy was the product of members of an older shamanic culture upon which the Confucian value system had been imposed from above. Prior to the imposition of Zhou institutions, these people would have had no reason to be reflective about the ways followed in their culture. Even today, people who have not been exposed to life in another culture assume that many forms of behavior that are the product of cultural learning are simply the natural way to do things, the only possible way to do things. They do so merely because the practices in which they were raised are so universally followed that they are never questioned.

Once the old society changed and social dislocations occurred, these people in ancient China must have been driven to question how it was that things had changed, and why it was that certain aspects of their society grew worse. The most beautiful flowerings of this process of inquiry are the *Lao Zi* and the *Zhuang Zi*. I do not want to belabor the point, nor do I want to create the impression that I think that Chinese society was the only one in which major social changes led to the development of critiques of society and to philosophical inquiry. I do want the reader to consider that if the criticisms that arose because of this process had any validity, then the Confucians would have been encouraged to review their own practices and expand their own thought.

The perceived value of human beings is another way in which Daoist and Confucian thinking are different, and this is, in a sense, a more fundamental difference than those mentioned in the previous paragraphs.

The Confucian thinkers believed that human beings have a position of unique value in the world. Heaven was concerned that the world be preserved as a good environment for human beings. Heaven wanted the political institutions of China to work for the benefit of the ordinary people. The ruler was called the Son of Heaven, meaning that he was the one chosen by Heaven to be its steward on earth. As the Son of Heaven, the ruler had a status second to none below heaven. Human beings (i.e., citizens of China) were superior to barbarians, and barbarians were superior to animals.

The Daoists, on the other hand, put human beings and everything else on the same level. The intrinsic value of a human being is no greater than the intrinsic value of a garden slug. So there is no sense that the world has been created for, or preserved for, or tended for human beings. It is just as much an ideal breeding place for mosquitoes and flies as it is a world suitable for human habitation.

In the *Great Learning* (*Da Xue* 大學) and the *Doctrine of the Mean* (*Zhong Yong* 中庸), the Confucians augment original Confucianism to incorporate some Daoist ideas and to answer some Daoist criticisms, but they do not depart from the fundamental Confucian perception that the world has been set aside for the benefit of human beings.

World-View of the *Great Learning* and *Doctrine of the Mean*

Original Zhou Religious and Social Beliefs Retained

Both the *Great Learning* and the *Doctrine of the Mean* quote the two most ancient Chinese books, the *Book of Odes* and the *Book of Documents*. Both of these texts contain references to the account of the rise of the Zhou dynasty according to which Heaven withdrew its mandate to rule from the rulers of the previous dynasty, the Shang, because those rulers had ceased to follow the will of Heaven, had become cruel and corrupt, and had ceased to benefit the people. The books warned the Zhou dynasty rulers that they too would lose their right to rule if they should ever follow in the footsteps of the Shang rulers.

Confucius established for Chinese scholars the position of interpreters and elucidators of the will of Heaven to the ruler. After Confucius, people in China no longer saw the Son of Heaven as the only one mediating between them and Heaven. Instead, it was the scholar-officials, the knight-scholars (*shi* 士), who had the primary responsibility for learning about the will of Heaven. The function of the ruler was seen to be to rule and to administer after having received appropriate guidance from those specialists. The dignity and power of the sovereign stayed with the king (and later the emperor), but a significant element of control had been appropriated by the knight-scholars. Confucius was the first one to take up the position of the independent teacher whose job it was to prepare individuals for service in government.

The Confucianism of Mencius

Mencius transformed the worldview of the Chinese still further by teaching how one might know the will of Heaven by the practice of introspection. He taught that Heaven's will is manifested in the world not only through portents and through the use of various forms of divination such as the *Yi Jing* (*Book of Changes*), but that the will of Heaven is also present in us as a kind of inner moral compass. At 7A:1, Mencius says that if one knows one's *xing* 性 (nature, innate axiological characteristics) then one knows Heaven.

Mencius believed that as regards their moral tendencies human beings are all essentially the same at birth and that the reason some people behave better or worse than others is that their experiences have either brought fulfillment to their innate moral potential (*xing*) or else have frustrated or even degraded it.

Whenever we graph any human characteristic, we find that most people cluster around an intermediate value, and then for greater or lesser values, the numbers progressively diminish the farther we go from the average. But at least as regards the strengths of certain moral impulses, Mencius says that while there may be minor differences everyone is essentially the same. So if he were to graph the strength of one of these moral impulses, he would show a rather level graph near the center that then falls abruptly to zero on either end. Mencius basically ignored the existence of atypical humans, or at least of humans who are atypical by reason of not sharing in the moral impulses in which he was interested.

Mencius would claim, I believe, that no human being is naturally inclined to kill other human beings, and that when a human being does commit homicide it is because of some major problem that has thwarted his development into a fully functioning person. But the Daoists, and particularly Zhuang Zi, are much more accurate in their portrayals of human beings because they take account of atypical individuals.

Da Xue – Zhong Yong Confucianism Has Been Influenced by the Daoist Critique

While Mencius thought that all human beings were essentially beneficent in their relations with other people and did evil only as a result of lack of proper nurture or of the operation of inimical environmental forces, Zhuang Zi saw immense variability in the innate characteristics of human beings. To put the argument in more modern terms, Mencius saw human beings as having one genotype with a very limited range of variability that can produce a range of phenotypes that is itself relatively limited but large enough to account for ordinarily observed behavioral problems. Zhuang Zi, however, saw humans as having a genotype with a high range of variability that can produce a range of phenotypes capable of manifesting an extremely wide range of behaviors, some of which are terrifying.

The *Zhuang Zi* (4:54/91) describes the son of Duke Ling of the state of Wei, saying: "His *de* (virtue, power) is by nature to kill," or, following a more traditional interpretation, "His virtue is naturally of a very low caliber." (*Qi de tian sha* 其德天殺 。) I believe that Zhuang Zi meant that this person's innate characteristics were such that he would readily kill other humans. Indeed, Zhuang Zi says that the means for dealing with such a person are comparable to the devices necessary for training tigers. He sees no possibility of reforming such an individual. All that can be done is to treat him in the same way one would treat any fierce beast — not in an inhumane way, but in such a way as to take his innate viciousness into full account.

Da Xue – Zhong Yong Confucianism Shows a Strong Mencian Influence

Although the authors of the *Great Learning* and the *Doctrine of the Mean* respond in various ways to the Daoist critique, the primary source of the philosophies expressed in these books is the *Mencius*. Material in *Mencius*, 4A:12, appears also in sections 20 and 23 of the *Doctrine of the Mean*. Although tradition says that Mencius quoted from the *Doctrine of the Mean*, the passages in the latter text seem to me to have rewritten the material in the *Mencius*, editing it slightly and, in the case of the material in section 23, adding significantly to it.

Da Xue - Zhong Yong **Thought Continues Confucius's Idea of Preparing Students for Government Service**

For the modern Western reader, one of the somewhat disconcerting elements of the thought of the *Great Learning* and the *Doctrine of the Mean* is that much attention is given to stating justifications for maintaining social stability and limiting social mobility. However, the expression of these values must have made these books appealing to the rulers of that time. One does not find much of this kind of thing in the works of Mencius, although Confucius does advise people at one point (*Analects*, 8:15) that one who does not hold a certain government office should not try to make policy for that office.

Teachings of Confucius and Mencius that Lie Behind the *Da Xue - Zhong Yong* Philosophy

The title of the *Doctrine of the Mean* and the impulse for writing that book may well come from the *Analects, 6:27*, where Confucius says that the Mean typifies the highest virtue, and adds that people are seldom able to maintain themselves at the Mean for long.

Confucius argued that compulsion by means of government regulation and legal punishment leads to attempts on the part of the people to avoid the coercion, and that in the process, they lose all sense of shame for the wrongful things that they may do. (See the *Analects*, 2:3.)

Confucius taught that our moral vision can become obscured. At 4:7, he says that the mistakes people make are influenced by the specific kinds of people that they are, and at 17:8 he points out that even good characteristics, such as benevolence, can lead us to do bad things when their action or expression is not modified by study and learning and is not mediated by a sound contextual understanding of events.

At 12:16, Confucius teaches that people could influence others to augment their good points or increase their debilities or bad points.

Confucius indicates that there is a process through which one comes closer and closer to the Dao of Heaven. At 2:4, he traces in his own life the steps through which he gradually integrated his own will so that it conformed with that of Heaven. His progress began at an early age when he aspired to study and learn, was carried through several stages by which he gradually learned more and more about the world in which he lived and also by which he reduced uncertainties and inconsistencies in his thinking, and finally arrived at a stage wherein his will was entirely harmonized with that of Heaven.

Mencius: Four Beginnings ——> Four Virtues

While it is sometimes said that Mencius affirms the nature of human beings to be good, it is more accurate to say that he teaches that by virtue of their innate constitutions, human beings are fully capable of **becoming** good. According to Mencius, human beings are born possessing the Four Beginnings (*si duan* 四端). These Four Beginnings are innate inclinations to react in certain way to significant events in the world. They amount to moral drives. But like the other drives for satisfying hunger, etc., human beings have to learn how to act in the real world so as to satisfy them. When and if the Four Drives become adequately developed, their operations are called the Four Virtues, which are: benevolence (*ren* 仁), sense of right and wrong (*yi* 義), sense of propriety or sense of ritual (*li* 禮), and wisdom (*zhi* 知, i.e., the ability to make objective analyses of the rightness and wrongness of the others' actions).

The Four Virtues Can Subordinate the Other Drives

Mencius believes that only the Four Virtues, or at least the potential for developing them, keep human beings from being no better than beasts. (See the *Mencius*, 4B:19.) When a person knows how to fully employ his total being (*jian shen* 踐身), he can do so because he has learned through living how to put all of the non-ethical drives at the service of the ethical drives. (See the *Mencius*, 7A:38.)

Mencius Does Not Give Very Detailed Directions for Becoming a Fully-Functioning Human Being

Mencius says: "As for their natures, human beings can become good" (see 6A:6), but what needs to be done to actually become good? On this score, Mencius is not very informative. He suggests that protection of the tender sprouts of moral sensitivity is necessary, implies that a person must continually will to do good, and suggests that both moral sloth and inimical external forces may inhibit the growth of these potentials to become a fully human being. However, he does not give the kind of specifics that would enable one not involved in his school or in his immediate tradition to confidently and successfully pursue a course of activities intended to bring his or her full powers to fruition as Mencius would have it.

Integration of Functions of the Mind is Advocated by the Authors of Both the *Great Learning* and the *Doctrine of the Mean*

Except for the translation of the *Doctrine of the Mean* by Gu Hong-ming, the translations of these two books which I have seen have all tried to express the meaning of the Chinese word "*cheng* 誠" by using "sincerity." To my way of thinking, that word does not give a very satisfactory understanding of *cheng* because it is possible for one to have two very **sincere** ideas about things and yet have these ideas be mutually contradictory. Discovery that one holds contradictory ideas about things can lead to a re-thinking of the issues involved, and that may lead to a higher degree of integration of thought, providing that the contradiction can be resolved. Since the completion of such a process of reconciliation of ideas appears to be the goal of these two books, I prefer to use "integration" to render it in English.

How Integration Is Necessary in the Process of Becoming a Fully Functioning, Moral Person

The Myth of Yu

In the myth of Yu, the Chinese established the belief that there is nothing evil about human nature — that evil comes about when natural human impulses are not permitted to find appropriate expression. That belief has lain largely hidden from explicit comment and investigation but has remained immensely potent in the daily lives of the Chinese people from before the time of Confucius down to the present.

The myth of Yu, found in various early sources and mentioned in the *Mencius*, tells how a great flood threatened all beneath heaven. The Lord on High looked down upon the earth and saw that the rising waters were driving poisonous snakes, as well as human beings, to high ground. Wanting to save the people he had created from harm, the Lord on High selected Gun to try to control the floods. Gun attempted to dam the waters at their sources. But the inevitable result of such an approach is that the water will eventually top the dams, and when it does so the dams will be suddenly carried away, releasing immense cataracts and causing far greater damage than originally might have been done. So Heaven withdrew its trust from Gun and even punished him for what he had done. Next Heaven called on Gun's son, Yu, to attempt the same task. With the help of a dragon, who performed the service of aerial surveyor, Yu constructed drainage ditches and deepened the channels of existing waterways, thus allowing the waters to flow harmlessly to the sea. By so doing, Yu provided ways in which the waters could be beneficial to human beings.[1]

Applied to human motivations, the obvious import of this myth is that it is dangerous to suppress human drives and beneficial to channel them so that they are fully vented in socially useful directions. The myth remained

1. See Derk Bodde's study and retelling of this myth in Samuel Noah Kramer's *Mythologies of the Ancient World*, pp. 398-402.

active in the background of the culture, but optimism about human nature did not survive untouched for long.

The Developments Before the *Great Learning* and the *Doctrine of the Mean*

Earlier sections of this introduction have already discussed the report given by Confucius of his own gradual transformation into someone who could do exactly as he willed without contravening the will of Heaven. Mencius continued the philosophical tradition of Confucius and also made reference to the much earlier myth of Yu. On his own, Mencius made acute observations of human behavior and formulated the conclusion that there is a biological basis for altruistic human behavior. He theorized that human beings have four different kinds of ethical impulse, or what we might call ethical drives, and argued that by depending on these moral drives, human beings are able to subordinate their more primitive drives and put their whole beings in the service of their highest moral impulses. The philosophers who wrote the *Great Learning* and the *Doctrine of the Mean* were concerned to formulate more carefully the disciplines through which people may become fully actualized moral agents, having sufficient coordination of all of their capabilities to enable them to become fully autonomous, unswayed by outside forces or transient internal impulses. That degree of coordination requires what the *Doctrine of the Mean* calls balance or equilibrium and harmony.

A Second Look at the Terms *Zhong* and *He*

In my translation I have used the words "balance" and "harmony" to convey the general meaning of these terms. It seems to me that these two words imply a view of the world and the human interactions that occur in it that may be too static. I think it is correct to say that for the thinkers in this tradition, it was not considered sufficient to simply be a certain kind of person. Rather, it was considered essential that one should be able to adapt to a moving and changing set of social interactions, much as a judo contestant seeks to maintain his own balance when competing with an opponent. What the *Doctrine of the Mean* literally says in the fourth paragraph of the first section is that when our emotions "have issued forth and all hit the middle of the section, the resulting state is called harmony." Viewed statically, this sounds like the author is saying that in planning any action, one should always determine the positive and negative extremes to which one's response should go and choose the mean between them.

If one were to conceive the problem in a static way and always to choose the mean value between the extremes of possible response, then, in most cases, one's actions would be inappropriate. For instance, possible responses to a young person's stealing a car might be the death penalty at one extreme and no penalty at the other extreme. So on that basis, someone might determine the appropriate first-offense penalty to be a fifty-year prison sentence. Of course, not only the penalty but even the assumptions and calculations needed to arrive at it are ridiculous. The point is one that is frequently made in our culture: Choosing a compromise position between extremes does not guarantee an appropriate response.

In section six I have again stayed close to the actual words of the text, but let us apply a dynamic view to the methodology attributed to the sage emperor Shun. The text says that he took "cognizance of the extremes and used their mean in governing the people." This sounds very much like the approach I attacked in the paragraph above. But consider also what is said in section four: two instances are mentioned in which people either fail by exceeding or fail by failing to come up to what is appropriate. Once more, the text sounds rather static. It sounds as though the Dao is something like a Platonic idea, or like a target of some kind, and as though one could metaphorically shoot arrows at it that might miss it by either carrying too far or by not carrying far enough. But the Dao is the total process of the universe, not a static standard for other things.

Let us view, in a dynamic sense, the idea of either exceeding or failing to reach something and ask how that idea applies to the results that someone might try to attain in a social situation. Suppose that a modern-day

Confucian judge examines the histories of a similar set of first offenders, each one of whom committed car theft. Some offenders were punished very severely, and some were punished very leniently. In many cases the offenders continued a life of crime after their release. It is hard to avoid the conclusion that in some cases society has gone too far in punishment and in other cases it has not gone far enough.

The job of the good judge then becomes to determine how much of what kind of response to the offense is enough to alter behavior in a desirable direction. Too great a response may be interpreted as the punitive action of an unjust society (the big gang), and too small a response may be viewed as the continued neglect of an indifferent society (the big dysfunctional family).

The reader has probably already objected that the histories, and therefore the likely reactions, of all of these offenders must be different, and so there can be no standard response that will prove effective. The implications of this observation are twofold: first, that an accurate, unbiased understanding must form the basis of any good judgment, and second, that such an understanding can probably be formed only dynamically, by interacting with the offender.

Maintaining Psycho-Physical Coordination Also Implies Eliminating Dissonance of Ideas

Once we have gone beyond the idea that there can be simplistic definitions of events that have any useful meaning, we are faced with the real necessity of figuring out the world and all of its intricacies. Like it or not, getting people to stop stealing cars, or stopping any other social problem, cannot be accomplished by any simple recipe-book approach. We must understand the social dynamics that produce social problems, and we must learn to influence those dynamics in beneficial ways.

One useful indication that we have not figured the world out completely is given when we discover contradictions in our account of it. If the world is a consistent whole and our ideas are inconsistent, then something must be wrong with our ideas. So discovery of logical problems with our verbal picture of the world should lead us back to a renewed process of discovery directed toward that world and reflected in a revised description of it.

The main section of the *Great Learning* says that one should "extend knowledge" (*zhi zhi* 致知) and that that goal is to be achieved by "investigating things" (*ge wu* 格物). There has been much discussion and controversy about what these words mean. I think that the word "things" should be construed as broadly as possible. Investigating these many things is then a process of forming a coherent account of the universe and the interactions that occur within it. This process of investigation is intended to bring eventual integrity to one's thoughts. The work of forming a coherent objective picture of the world does not plumb the limits of one's task.

Triple Consistency Check: Internal-Internal, Internal-External, and Global

I think that in the view of the authors of the *Great Learning* and the *Doctrine of the Mean,* it would not be sufficient to have an approach to the world that is scientifically accurate and logically correct. As I have indicated above, the authors of these books probably had in mind the idea of what we would call a scientific account of the world. The main difference would perhaps be that, with the Daoist critique in mind, they would be less certain about the possibility of forming a static set of concepts that would allow them to accurately operate in the world. They were very much interested, I believe, in the dynamic and changing aspects of things. But there is another reason that science would not have completely satisfied them.

Because they were in the tradition of Mencius, they must have been convinced that positive social impulses are part of the biological inheritance of all human beings, or at least of all that have not been damaged in some way. Their awareness of other motivations shared by human beings, such as the fear, greed, anger, and other emotions. that can operate in anti-social ways, would necessarily have been sharpened by reading the works of the more authoritarian Confucian scholar, Xun Zi. They would have been aware that any action that a human being initiates involves a resolution or balancing out of all the motivational forces acting on that person.

One's motivations may be good, but success is not guaranteed because one does something in accord with those good motivations. One may act out of a true sense of duty and do just the wrong thing because one has inadequately understood the social situation and what is really needed to productively influence the people within it. Or, one may have a sincere love for someone else and fail to react against something bad that they do because one is blinded by one's love. Moving beyond the level of Mencius's Four Beginnings of moral motivation to the corresponding mature accomplishments he calls the Four Virtues necessarily involves conscious interaction with one's social environment, and it also involves monitoring one's own responses so that one becomes aware of, and can compensate for, any potential emotional biases in one's reactions to interactions with others.

So the truly moral agent in the world must be a person who has mastered himself or herself — not in the sense that one has suppressed any part of oneself, but in the sense that one has learned the highest form of coordination, wherein all impulses, motivations, drives, etc. are fluidly interactive and responsive to the human will that oversees them all, takes direction **from** them all, and makes sure that the actions taken are actually responsive to the world and productive of the changes the actions were intended to produce.

One of my Chinese friends, whom I will not name for fear of embarrassing him, once observed to me that American people seemed to him significantly different from the people among whom he had grown up in one respect: they often cheerfully accepted flaws in themselves, evinced no intention to try to change what they realized were damaging characteristics, and passed the whole matter off by observing: "We all have our little foibles." While I do not think that his observation is universally true, it does lead one to inquire why the Chinese may be more willing and more eager to attempt to transform themselves into better people than was their lot according to the dice thrown by genetics, early family life, and general social environment. Perhaps the reader may find some of the answers in these two little books.

THE BOOKS THEMSELVES

The Question of Authorship

Actually, nobody can know for sure who the authors of these two books were. Song dynasty scholars held that the *Great Learning* was the work of either Master Zeng, a disciple of Confucius, or Zi-si, the grandson of Confucius. Tradition holds that Zi-si wrote the *Doctrine of the Mean*. There is no real evidence for any of these assertions, and there is much indirect evidence, particularly in the *Doctrine of the Mean*, that they were written during the Qin dynasty, the period of disunity between the Qin and the Han, or the early Han dynasty.

The traditional attributions would then place the authors as having lived between the time of Confucius and the time of Mencius, but the language in which these two books are written is much more modern than the language of the *Mencius*. Moreover, certain passages that appear in the *Mencius* in a somewhat murky style appear also in the *Doctrine of the Mean* in a style that appears to me to have been edited for clarity of structure and intelligibility of vocabulary. Moreover, although Mencius and Zhuang Zi were contemporaries, there is no clear indication that the thought of either was influenced by that of the other or that either criticized the other or responded to something that the other had said, nor does the *Mencius* make any other obvious reference to the critique of

Confucianism made by the Daoists. The thought of the *Great Learning* and the *Doctrine of the Mean* seems both to build on what Mencius taught, to respond to some of the criticisms the Daoists leveled against Confucianism, and to incorporate many Daoist positions.

I believe it is best to say that the authors were anonymous Confucian scholars living sometime between the last years of the Zhou dynasty and the early years of the Han dynasty, and that the authors were sympathetic to the thought of Mencius and desired to recommend Confucianism of this variety to whomever would rule China from their time on.

The Texts

There are no great problems with the characters used to write these texts. Since both texts are relatively down-to-earth, context has been enough to assure that the text was transmitted with correct characters. There are some variations between characters used in the present-day version of the *Book of Odes* (*Shi Jing*) and quotations therefrom that appear in these books, but I have left those characters as they appear in the present-day texts of the *Great Learning* and *Doctrine of the Mean*.

Both texts appear in the *Li Ji* 禮記, from which they were excerpted for individual publication and for inclusion in the *Four Books* (*Si Shu* 四書) established by the Song dynasty scholar Zhu Xi 朱熹 (1130–1200 A.D.). My translation follows the latter versions. In the case of the *Doctrine of the Mean*, only the division into sections is different. I have provided the original section numbers for the benefit of readers who would like to compare the two texts, or who wish to refer to translations that follow the *Li Ji* section numbering. Zhu Xi edited the *Great Learning*, however, and rearranged the sequence of the text. The original text found in the *Li Ji* is not divided into sections, so I have provided information on the sequence of the original text.

TRANSLATION
OF
THE
GREAT LEARNING

經第一章

The Main Section

大學之道在明明德，在親民，在止
於至善。知止而后有定，定而后能
靜，靜而后能安，安而后能慮，慮
而后能得。物有本末，事有終始，
知所先後，則近道矣。

{*Li Ji* segment 1} The course of action (dao) set out as the Great Learning consists of burnishing one's bright virtue, loving the people, and abiding in the highest goodness. When one knows wherein to abide, then there is certainty. When there is certainty, one can be tranquil. When one is tranquil, one can find peace. When one is at peace, one can think. When one can think, one can get it. Creatures have their roots and branches. Events have their beginnings and endings. If one knows what is before and what comes after, one is getting close to the Dao.

古之欲明明德於天下者，先治其國
；欲治其國者，先齊其家；欲齊其
家者，先修其身；欲修其身者，先
正其心；欲正其心者，先誠其意；
欲誠其意者，先致其知；致知在格
物。物格而后知至，知至而后意誠
，意誠而后心正，心正而后身修，

身修而后家齊，家齊而后國治，國
治而后天下平。

In antiquity, those who desired to burnish bright virtue throughout the
world first governed their own countries. Those who desired to govern
their countries first regulated their own families. Those who desired to
regulate their families first cultivated their own characters. Those who
desired to cultivate their characters first made their own minds upright.
Those who desired to make their minds upright first brought integrity to
their own thoughts. Those who desired to bring integrity to their thoughts
first extended their knowledge. Extending knowledge lies in investigating
things. After things have been investigated, knowledge is carried to its
limit. After knowledge is carried to its limit, one's thoughts can be
integrated. After one's thoughts are integrated, the mind can be made
upright. After the mind is made upright, one's character can be cultivated.
After one's character is cultivated, one's family can be regulated. After
one's family is regulated, one's country can be well governed. After one's
country is well governed, the world can be made to be at peace.

自天子以至於庶人，壹是皆以修身
爲本。其本亂而末治者否矣；其所
厚者薄，而其所薄者厚，未之有也
。

From the Son of Heaven down to the multitudes, each and every person
takes cultivating his character as his fundamental task. If the (roots =) fun-
daments be disordered it is impossible that the (tips =) peripheral matters
should be well ordered. If what should be substantial is pared down, it is
impossible that what originally ought to have been comparatively slight
would then become substantial. {For *LJ* segment 2 go to section 5.}.

COMMENTARY: In the last two sentences the author refers to the question whether one should concentrate on the remote goals of world peace, etc. to the detriment of the development of one's own character and other such issues.

傳十章

The Ten Explanatory Sections:

一 釋明明德

Section One

(Explaining burnishing bright virtue)

唐誥曰：『克明德。』大甲曰：『
顧諟天之明命。』帝典曰：『克明
峻德。』皆自明也。

{5} The "Announcement of Kang" [the Kang Gao chapter of the *Book of Documents*] says: "[King Wen] was able to burnish his virtue."

The "Tai-jia" [chapter of the *Book of History*] says: "He saw this bright Mandate of Heaven."

The "Di Dian" [the "Yao Dian" chapter of the *Book of History*] says: "He was able to burnish [his] lofty virtue."

All of these instances refer to self (burnishing =) cultivation.

二　釋新民

Section Two

(Explaining renewing the people)

湯之盤銘曰：『苟日新，日日新，
又日新。』康誥曰：『作新民。』
詩曰：『周雖舊邦，其命維新。』
是故，君子無所不用其極。

The engraving on the wash basin of Tang (founder of the Shang dynasty) says: "If you renew yourself daily, then day after day you will be renewed, and yet once again will you be renewed."

The "Announcement of Kang" [the Kang Gao chapter of the *Book of Documents*] says: "Arouse the process of renewal in the people."

The *Book of Odes* says: "Although the Zhou is an old nation, its mandate to rule is maintained[1] fresh."[2]

So the morally noble man always uses his best efforts on everything.

1. The character that is translated as "maintained" here probably did not have that meaning in the poem, but was rather a word added for euphony. When quoted here, however, the author probably intended the character's present meaning to be understood.
2. Poem number 235 in the arrangement of the *Shi Jing* given by the Han dynasty scholar Mao Heng.

三　釋止于至善

Section Three

(Explaining abiding in the highest good)

詩云：『邦畿千里，惟民所止』。
詩云：『緡蠻黃鳥，止于丘隅。』
子曰：『於止，知其所止，可以人
而不如鳥乎？』

The *Book of Odes* says: "The royal domain of a thousand miles is where the people abide."[3] The *Book of Odes* says: "How well preened and resplendent is the yellow bird; it abides on the crook of the hill."[4] The Master said: "With regard to abiding, it knows where to abide. Is it possible that people should not be the equals of birds in this respect?"

詩云：『穆穆文王，於緝熙敬止。
』爲人君，止於仁；爲人臣，止於
敬；爲人子，止於孝；爲人父，止
於慈；與國人交，止於信。

The *Book of Odes* says: "How reverent was King Wen. He abided in and extended respectfulness."[5] As a ruler of men, he abided in benevolence. As a minister, he abided in respect. As a son, he abided in filial piety. As a

3. Mao number 303.
4. Mao number 230.
5. Mao number 235.

father, he abided in compassion. In interacting with the people of the country, he abided in trustworthiness. {*Li Ji* segment 6 is in section 4.}

詩云：『瞻彼淇澳，菉竹猗猗；有
斐君子，如切如磋，如琢如磨；瑟
兮僩兮，赫兮喧兮；有斐君子，終
不可諠兮。』如切如磋者，道（導）
學也；如琢如磨者，自修也；瑟兮
僩兮者，恂慄也；赫兮喧兮者，威
儀也；有斐君子，終不可諠兮者，
道盛德至善，民之不能忘也。

{4} The *Book of Odes* says: "See that bank of the river Qi, so thick with verdant bamboo. The elegant nobleman, as though cut and polished, as though carved and burnished. Sober and stern, imposing and thunderous; the elegant nobleman can never be forgotten."[6] "As though cut and polished" refers to leading someone to learn. "As though carved and burnished" refers to self-cultivation. "Sober and stern" refers to his awesomeness. "Imposing and thunderous" refers to his grandeur. "The elegant nobleman can never be forgotten" refers to the fact that his dao is flourishing, his virtue is of the highest degree of goodness, and so the people cannot forget him.

詩云：『於戲！前王不忘。』君子
賢其賢而親其親，小人樂其樂而利
其利，此以沒世不忘也。

6. Mao number 55.

The *Book of Odes* says: "Ah! The former king will never be forgotten."[7] [This means that] the morally noble man will treat with high respect those whom the former king found worthy, and will remain affectionate to those whom the former king loved. The common people will enjoy what the former king took joy in, and will derive benefit from what the former kings found to be beneficial. Therefore, the former king can never be forgotten [since his value judgments are passed down by tradition both among the elite and the common people]. {*Li Ji* segment 5 is in section 1.}

四 釋本末

Section Four

(Explaining root and tips)

子曰：『聽訟，吾猶人也；必也使
無訟乎！』無情者不得盡其辭，大
畏民志：此謂知本。

{6} The Master said: "In trying cases I am like everyone else. [But] I would cause there to be no need for litigation!" To not permit those who do not tell the truth to finish their arguments [having established that their premises are wrong], and to have the highest respect for the aspirations of the common people[8] — this is what is meant by "knowing [the roots =] fundamentals." {*Li Ji* segment 7 is in section 7.}

7. Mao number 269.
8. See Lao Zi, *Dao De Jing,* section 20.

五　釋格物致知

Section Five

(Explaining investigation of things and extension of knowledge)

此謂知本。此謂知之至也。

{2} This is spoken of as knowing the root. This is spoken of as knowledge being carried to its limit. {*Li Ji* segment 3 is in section 6.}

《所謂致知在格物者，言欲致吾之知，在即物而窮其理也。蓋人心之靈，莫不有知，而天下之物，莫不有理；惟於理有未窮，故其知有所不盡也。是以大學始教，必使學者即凡天下之物，莫不因其已知之理而益窮之，以求至乎其極。至於用力之久，而一旦豁然貫通焉，則眾物之表裡精粗無不到，而吾心之全體大用無不明矣。此謂物格，此謂知之至也。》

(The following passage was written by the Song dynasty philosopher, Zhu Xi 朱熹 (1130-1200), to try to maintain the continuity of this book by supplying the general meaning of the chapter he believed to be missing.)

<<The words "Extending knowledge lies in investigating things" mean that if I desire to extend my knowledge then I must direct my attention to things and exhaustively understand their *li* (patterns, "principles"). This foregoing is so because the spiritual responsiveness of all human minds has awareness and knowledge, and all of the things of the world have *li*. It is only where the *li* of things have not been exhaustively understood that one's knowledge lacks exhaustiveness. For this reason, when the *Great Learning* begins teaching it must cause the student to address himself to all of the things of the world and in each case to base himself on what he already knows of the *li* and to continue to deepen his understanding until he arrives at a terminal point. After one has exerted himself for a long time, then one day everything will suddenly click into place so that the external and internal aspects, the coarse and the fine structures of the multitude of things will all be included in a higher synthesis, and the greater function of my entire mind will not fail to be clear in its perceiving. This is spoken of as things being investigated and knowledge being perfected.>>

(End of Zhu Xi's emendation)

六 釋誠意

Section Six

(Explaining integrating thought)

所謂『誠其意』者，毋自欺也。如
惡惡臭，如好好色，此之謂自謙。

故君子必慎其獨也。小人閒居爲不
善，無所不至：見君子而后厭然揜
其不善而著其善；人之視己，如見
其肺肝然，則何益矣？此謂誠於中
，形於外。故君子必慎其獨也。

{3} "Bringing integrity to one's thoughts" means not to have any self-deception. It is like the state that exists when one hates a bad smell or is attracted by a pleasant sexual stimulus. That state is called self-consistency. So the morally noble man must be careful of the times when he is alone [lest he do something to put himself in conflict with himself and thus create an internal inconsistency or conflict]. When left by himself the petty person will do things that are bad, and he will stop at nothing. When he sees a morally noble man he will cover up his bad deeds while acting in a servile manner and trying to exhibit his good deeds. But when people look at [that petty person], it is as though they can see his lungs and liver, so what good is [his attempt to dissemble]? The foregoing is to say that when there is an uncontradicted, integral state within, it must take form externally [in the behavior, non-verbal communications, etc. of the person]. Therefore, the morally noble man must be careful of himself during his periods of solitude. {*Li Ji* segment 4 is in section 3.}

曾子曰：『十目所視，十手所指，
其嚴乎！』富潤屋，德潤身，心廣
體胖。故君子必誠其意。

Master Zeng said: "What ten eyes see and ten hands point to is a serious matter." Wealth is seen in the magnificence of one's dwellings, but virtue is seen in the quality of one's person. If one's mind is unharried one's body will be at ease. Therefore the morally noble man must integrate his thoughts.

七 釋正心修身

Section Seven

(Explaining making the mind upright and cultivating the character)

所謂『修身在正其心』者，身有所
忿懥，則不得其正；有所恐懼，則
不得其正；有所好樂，則不得其正
；有所憂患，則不得其正。心不在
焉：視而不見，聽而不聞，食而不
知其味。此謂『修身在正其心。』

{7} The teaching that "cultivating one's character lies in rectifying one's mind" means that if one's [mind] experiences any anger it will not be correct. If it has any fear then it will not be correct. If it has any desires then it will not be correct. If it has any worries then it will not be correct. When one does not have presence of mind then one will look without truly seeing, listen without truly hearing, eat without truly tasting. This is what is meant by saying that "Cultivating one's character lies in rectifying one's mind."

八 釋修身齊家

Section Eight

(Explaining cultivating one's character and regulating one's family)

所謂『齊其家在修其身』者，人之
其所親愛而辟焉，之其所賤惡而辟
焉，之其所畏敬而辟焉，之其所哀
矜而辟焉，之其所敖惰而辟焉。故
好而知其惡，惡而知其美者，天下
鮮矣。故諺有之曰：『人莫知其子
之惡，莫知其苗之碩。』此謂身不
修，不可以齊其家。

With regard to the teaching that "regulating one's family lies in cultivating one's character," [we may observe that]: People are biased with regard to what they love. They are biased in regard to what they loathe. They are biased in regard to what they hold in awe. They are biased where they feel sorrow. They are biased where they feel contempt. Therefore, few are those who like someone and yet know his evil side, or loathe someone and yet know his good points. Therefore there is an adage which says: "No one knows the evils of his sons, nor do they recognize the [ample] size of their grain sprouts." That explains why if one does not cultivate one's character, one cannot regulate one's family.

九 釋齊家治國

Section Nine

(Explaining regulating one's family and governing the nation)

所謂『治國必先齊其家』者，其家
不可教，而能教人者，無之。故君
子不出家，而成教於國。孝者，所
以事君也；弟者，所以事長也；慈
者，所以使眾也。康誥曰：『如保
赤子。』心誠求之，雖不中，不遠
矣。未有學養子而后嫁者也。

The teaching that "in order to govern the country one must first regulate one's family" means that there is no one who can teach [other] people if he cannot teach his own family. Therefore the morally noble man establishes his teaching in the country even before he leaves his family. Filial piety is what it takes to serve one's sovereign. Brotherly love is what it takes to serve one's elders. Compassion is what it takes to employ the multitudes. The *"Kang Gao"* (the "Announcement of Kang" chapter of the *Book of History*) says: "[It is] like protecting a newborn baby." If one's mind seeks [for what is needed by a baby] with integrity of purpose, even though one may miss the target one will not be far off. There are none who first study how to rear children and then get married.

一家仁，一國興仁；一家讓，一國
興讓，一人貪戾，一國作亂；其機
如此。此謂一言僨事，一人定國。
堯舜帥天下以仁，而民從之；桀紂
帥天下以暴，而民從之。其所令反
其所好，而民不從。是故君子有諸
己，而后求諸人；無諸己，而后非
諸人。所藏乎身不恕，而能喻諸人
者，未之有也。故治國在齊其家。

If one family is truly benevolent, then the country will become benevolent. If one family truly is yielding then the whole country will become yielding. If one person is greedy and violent, the whole country will fall into civil disorder. The motivating factors are all like this. This is what is meant by saying that one word can ruin everything, and one man can stabilize the country. Yao and Shun ruled the world with benevolence, and the people emulated them. [The evil emperors] Jie and Zhou ruled the world with violence, and the people emulated them. Should what the rulers' command go against what the people desire, then the people will not follow them. Therefore, the morally noble man demands of others only what he has within himself, and denies to others only what he has eliminated from within himself. Without empathy, it is impossible that one should transmit to others what one has within oneself. So governing the country lies in regulating one's family.

詩云：『桃之夭夭，其葉蓁蓁，之
子于歸，宜其家人。』宜其家人，

而后可以教國人。詩云：『宜兄宜弟。』宜兄宜弟，而后可以教國人。詩云：『其儀不忒，正是四國。』其爲父子兄弟足法，而后民法之也。此謂治國在齊其家。

The *Book of Odes* says: "The peach trees are burgeoning, their foliage is luxuriant. When this youngster goes to her new home she will surely harmonize with her new family."[9] By harmonizing with one's family members, one can then teach the people of the country. The *Book of Odes* says: "[The noble man is] in harmony with his older and younger brothers."[10] By harmonizing with one's brothers one can then teach the people of the country. The *Book of Odes* says: "His demeanor was not incorrect, and so he rectified the countries on all four sides."[11] Only when one performs well enough as a father, son, older brother, and younger brother to serve as a model will the people model themselves on one. This is what is meant by saying that governing the country lies in regulating one's own family.

9. Mao number 6.
10. Mao number 173.
11. Mao number 152.

十 釋治國平天下

Section Ten

(Explaining governing the country and pacifying the world)

所謂『平天下在治其國』者，上老
老而民興孝；上長長而民興弟；上
恤孤而民不倍。是以君子有絜矩之
道也。所惡於上，毋以使下，所惡
於下，毋以事上；所惡於前，毋以
先後；所惡於後，毋以從前；所惡
於右，毋以交於左，所惡於左，毋
以交於右：此之謂絜矩之道。

When it says that "Pacifying the world lies in governing one's country" [it means that]: If those in power treat their aged with the respect due to the aged, then the people will come to display filial piety. If those in power treat their elders with the respect due to elders, then the people will come to display brotherly reverence. If those in power take pity on the orphaned, then the people will not become rebellious. Therefore the morally noble man has a dao [that includes an ethical standard to be used like] a carpenter's square: Do not use on your subordinates what you dislike in your superiors. Do not serve your superiors with what you dislike in your subordinates. Do not do to those behind you what you dislike having done to you by those in front of you. Do not do to those in front of you what you dislike having done by those behind you. Do not hand to the person on the left what you dislike [to receive from] the

person on the right. Do not hand to the person on the right what you
dislike [to receive from] the person on the left. This is called the dao like a
carpenter's square.

詩云：『樂只君子，民之父母。』
民之所好好之，民之所惡惡之，此
之謂民之父母。詩云：『節彼南山
，維石巖巖；赫赫師尹，民具爾瞻
。』有國者不可以不慎，辟則天下
僇矣！

The *Book of Odes* says: May the nobleman be joyful, [he is] the parent of
the people."[12] Like what the people like, dislike what the people dislike —
this is what is meant by being the parent of the people. The *Book of Odes*
says: "How tall that Mount Nan with its stones so craggy. How awesome
that Grand Tutor Yin. The people all gaze at him."[13] Those who hold
power in a country must be careful. If they should err to one side or the
other they would be despised by the world.

詩云：『殷之未喪師，克配上帝；
儀監于殷，峻命不易。』道得眾，
則得國；失眾，則失國。是故君子
先慎乎德。有德此有人，有人此有
土，有土此有財，有財此有用。德

12. Mao number 172
13. Mao number 191

者，本也；財者，末也。外本內末
，爭民施奪。是故財聚則民散，財
散則民聚。是故言悖而出者，亦悖
而入；貨悖而入者，亦悖而出。康
誥曰：『惟命不于常。』道善則得
之，不善則失之矣。楚書曰：『楚
國無以為寶，惟善以為寶。』舅犯
曰：『亡人無以為寶，仁親以為寶
。』

The *Book of Odes* says: "Before the Yin (i.e., Shang) dynasty lost the multitudes, it was a fit [earthly] counterpart to the Lord on High. It would be appropriate to mirror ourselves in the Yin — the Great Mandate is not an easy one [to keep]."[14] This is to say that if one gets the multitudes then one gets the country. If one loses the multitudes then one loses the country. For this reason the morally noble man is first careful with respect to [his own] virtue. If [a ruler] has virtue then he will have people. If he has people then he will have territory. If he has territory then he will have wealth. If he has wealth then he will have things to meet his needs. Virtue is the (root =) basis, and wealth is a (tip =) peripheral issue. If one casts out the basis and concentrates on obtaining the superficial, then one struggles against the people and employs plundering. For this reason, if wealth is concentrated then the people will disperse, whereas if wealth is distributed then the people will accumulate. Thus it is said that if words are spoken in a contrariwise manner then they will likewise return to one in a contrariwise manner. If goods are acquired in an abnormal manner, then they will leave one's hands in an abnormal manner as well. The

14. Mao number 235.

"Kang Gao" ("Announcement of Kang") says: "Oh, the Mandate is not constant." If one's dao is good, then one will get [the Mandate], but if it is not good, then one will lose [the Mandate]. The *Documents of Chu* says: "There is nothing that the state of Chu holds precious, except for the Good." Uncle Fan (maternal uncle of Duke Wen of the state of Jin 晉) said: "The exiled Duke held nothing precious except being benevolent to those who were dear to him."

秦誓曰：『若有一个臣，斷斷兮，無他技；其心休休焉，其如有容焉。人之有技，若己有之；人之彥聖，其心好之；不啻若自其口出，寔能容之，以能保我子孫黎民，尚亦有利哉！人之有技，媢嫉以惡之；人之彥聖，而違之俾不通；寔不能容，以不能保我子孫黎民，亦曰殆哉！』唯仁人放流之，迸諸四夷，不與同中國。此謂『唯仁人爲能愛人，能惡人。』見賢而不能舉，舉而不能先，命也；見不善而不能退，退而不能遠，過也。好人之所惡，惡人之所好，是謂拂人之性，菑必逮夫身。是故君子有大道，必忠信以得之，驕泰以失之。

The "*Qin Shi*" [the "Declaration of the Duke of Qin," a chapter of the *Shu Jing]* says: "If there were a minister who were most sincere but had no other skills, then providing that he was broadminded he might be retained. If there were one who regarded the possession of skills by others as though he himself possessed them, and who regarded the moral excellence of others with fond regard and did not just utter vain praises, then he should indeed be retained because he would be able to protect my descendants and the common people and would be truly beneficial. If there were one who hated others because of envy for their skills, and would therefore suppress them and cause them not to become well-known, that person could certainly not be retained because he would be unable to protect my descendents and the common people and could indeed be called a menace." A benevolent person would exile such a man among the four barbarian nations and not permit him to associate with the Chinese people. This is what was meant when [Confucius] said that "Only the benevolent man is both able to love people and to hate people."[15] If one finds a worthy person and is unable to give him a higher rank, or if he be given a higher rank but one cannot give him precedence, that is a question of the Mandate of Heaven. If one finds a person who is not good and does not retire him, or having retired him does not send him far away, that is a moral error. [For the ruler to] love what the people hate and hate what the people love is called being in opposition to the *xing* (natures) of the people, and those who do so must have calamity visited on their persons. For this reason, there is a great dao for the members of the nobility: By loyalty and trustworthiness one will certainly gain the people, by pride and arrogance one will certainly lose them.

生財有大道：生之者衆，食之者寡
；爲之者疾，用之者舒；則財恆足
矣。仁者以財發身，不仁者以身發

---

15. *Lun Yu* (*The Analects of Confucius*), 4.3

財。未有上好仁而下不好義者也；
未有好義，其事不終者也；未有府
庫財，非其財者也。

There is a great dao for the production of wealth: Those who produce
wealth must be many, and those who consume wealth must be few. Those
who do the work must be energetic and those who use [the resultant
products] must be restrained. In that case there will always be a
sufficiency of wealth. Benevolent people expend wealth to develop
themselves, and unbenevolent people expend themselves to produce
wealth. It has never been the case that when those who are the superiors
love benevolence those who are the subordinates fail to love their duties. It
has never been the case that when people love their duties they yet fail to
complete their responsibilities. There has never been wealth stored away
in depositories [anywhere in the country] that has not belonged [ultimately]
to the ruler.

孟獻子曰：『畜馬乘，不察於雞豚
；伐冰之家不畜牛羊；百乘之家，
不畜聚斂之臣；與其有聚斂之臣，
寧有盜臣。』此謂國不以利為利，
以義為利也。長國家而務財用者，
必自小人矣；彼為善之，小人之使
為國家，菑害並至，雖有善者，亦
無如之何矣。此謂『國不以利為利
，以義為利』也。

Master Meng Xian said: "Those who keep a fine team and carriage do not overly concern themselves with the chickens and piglets. Those families who can afford an ice-house do not raise cattle and sheep. A family commanding a hundred chariots does not keep ministers who make depredations on the people; rather than having ministers who make depredations on the people it would be better to have thieving ministers who would steal from the government coffers." This means that the nation does not take profit to be beneficial, but takes righteousness to be beneficial. Those who lead nations and yet take the accumulation of wealth to be their prime task must be under the sway of petty people. The fact that those [petty people] are taken to be good [is the reason that] those petty people are caused to handle the affairs of the nation. [Because of that state of affairs] calamities and natural disasters strike at the same time, and even if there are good people [in the government] they will be powerless to do anything to ameliorate the situation. This is what is meant by saying that "the nation does not take profit to be beneficial, but takes righteousness to be beneficial."

TRANSLATION
OF
THE
DOCTRINE OF THE
MEAN

第一章

天命之謂性，率性之謂道，修道之
謂教。道也者，不可須臾離也；可
離，非道也。是故，君子戒慎乎其
所不睹，恐懼乎其所不聞。莫見乎
隱，莫顯乎微，故君子慎其獨也。
喜怒哀樂之未發，謂之中；發而皆
中節，謂之和。中也者，天下之大
本也；和也者，天下之達道也。致
中和，天地位焉，萬物育焉。 *(LJ, 1¹)*

Section One

{*LJ*, 1¹} The *xing* (human nature) is what Heaven has called into existence within us through its mandate. To follow out this *xing* is called one's dao (way, course, process). To correct (*i.e.*, cultivate) the dao that one takes in life is called the process of education.

The Dao may not be left for an instant. If it were possible to leave it, it would not be the Dao. Therefore the morally noble man is careful [even] in regard to what he cannot be observed to do and wary [even] about what he cannot be heard to do.

1. The *Li Ji* version of the *Doctrine of the Mean* is virtually identical to the *Four Books* version, except for the way it is divided into sections. I give the corresponding section numbers.

There is nothing more obvious than what has been concealed and nothing more apparent than what is subtle. Therefore the morally noble man takes great care during those times when he is alone.

The state before delight, anger, sorrow, and joy are aroused is called equilibrium (*zhong* 中). When those emotions have issued forth and all of them do so in a measured (not extreme) way, [the resulting state] is called harmony (*he* 和).

Equilibrium (of the cosmic forces corresponding to human emotions) is the great root of the world. Harmony is the most excellent dao (way of functioning) of the world. When equilibrium and harmony reach their highest degree, then Heaven and Earth take their correct positions with respect to each other and the myriad creatures are fostered.

Commentary:

Note that the word dao is used in two senses in the above passage. This word's basic meaning is path or course, so any course that one may take in life can be called a dao. Each person has a set of innate characteristics and drives called a *xing*, and the Confucians believe that one's task in life is to help this *xing* find full expression in life. Nevertheless, one can act in ways that are not harmonious with one's innermost ethical impulses, and by doing so one also chooses a dao in life. So there is a need to cultivate and correct one's personal dao. On the other hand, there is a certain way that the Universe works, and that, too, is a dao. One's actions, when based on selfish desires, may cause one to choose a course that goes contrary to the way that the universe works, so there is the possibility of a conflict between one's personal dao, what one actually does, and the universal Dao. According to Confucians, the universe is a moral entity, so the mismatch between one's personal dao and the great Dao of the universe may be a moral conflict. The way to avoid such conflict is to follow the guidance of one's moral nature, one's *xing*. But the *xing* is not an instinct like the innate ability that some spiders have to weave orb webs. Rather, it is a more generalized drive that includes no specific instructions for action, like our hunger for food. We require to learn much before we are able to efficiently satisfy our hunger by consistently meeting our need for food.

The above passage also points to the existence of both an internal equilibrium and harmony and an external equilibrium and harmony that pertains to the whole universe. The cosmic forces that act to constitute the universe are analogous to the emotions that motivate human actions. Or, to put it another way, human feelings are instances of cosmic forces. The universe enjoys its immense creative energies because it is in balance and harmony with itself. So we too can only hope to emulate the productivity of the universe if we are able to come into a state of balance and harmony within ourselves and with our surroundings.

第二章

仲尼曰：『君子中庸，小人反中庸。君子之中庸也，君子而時中；小人之〔反〕中庸也，小人而無忌憚也。』 *(LJ, 2a)*

Section Two

{*LJ*, 2} Zhong-ni (Confucius) said: "The morally noble man keeps to the Mean (lit., he avoids extremes and keeps to the ordinary). The petty man does just the opposite." The avoidance of extremes and preference for the ordinary exhibited by the morally noble man is such that at all times he maintains his balance. The opposite tendency of the petty man is such that there is nothing which he restrains himself from doing.

Commentary:

The author immediately provides his readers with an example of how the individual may work at cross purposes to the dao by opposing his individual energies to the vast power of the universe.

第三章

子曰：中庸其至矣乎！民鮮能久矣
。

Section Three

The Master (*i.e.*, Confucius) said: "Oh, how far-reaching is the Mean. Seldom indeed are the people able to hold to it for long."

第四章

子曰：道之不行也，我知之矣：知
者過之，愚者不及也。道之不明也
，我知之矣：賢者過之，不肖者不
及也。人莫不飲食也。鮮能知味也
。 (*LJ*, 2b)

Section Four

The Master said: "I know why the Dao fails to be put into action. The intelligent ones exceed it and the unintelligent ones do not reach it. I know why people do not understand the Dao. The worthies exceed it, and the unworthy ones do not reach it. Everyone must eat and drink, but few are those who can know the flavors of what they consume."

第五章

子曰：『道其不行矣夫！』(*LJ*, 2c)

Section Five

The Master said: "Oh, how the Dao fails to be put into practice!"

第六章

子曰：『舜其大知也與！舜好問而好察邇言；隱惡而揚善，執其兩端，用其中於民，其斯以為舜乎！』
(*LJ*, 3)

Section Six

{*LJ*, 3} The Master said: "Great was the wisdom of [the sage emperor] Shun. Shun liked to ask questions and to investigate simple sayings. He concealed the evil [that others did] and called attention to their good deeds. Shun's way was to take cognizance of the extremes [defining the limits of any problem or the extremes in the views of other people] and use their mean in governing the people. It was by this very means that he became Shun."

第七章

子曰：『人皆曰「予知」；驅而納
諸罟，攫陷阱之中而莫之知辟也。
人皆曰「予知」；擇乎中庸而不能
期月守也。』 *(LJ,* 4)

Section Seven

{*LJ*, 4} The Master said: "People all say: 'I know.' But if they be pursued and caught in a net or trapped in a pitfall, then no one knows how to escape. People all say: 'I know.' But should they happen to choose the Mean [by acting in equilibrium and harmony], they would not be able to hold to it for even a whole month."

第八章

子曰：『回之爲人也，擇乎中庸，
得一善，則拳拳服膺而弗失之矣。
』 *(LJ,* 5a)

Section Eight

{*LJ*, 5} The Master said: "Hui's (*i.e.*, Yen Yuan's) characteristic way of doing things was to choose [from among courses of action the one characterized by] the Mean (equilibrium and harmony), and once having gotten one good thing [by this approach], he would clasp it tightly to his bosom and never let it go."

第九章

子曰：『天下國家可均也，爵祿可
辭也，白刃可蹈也，中庸不可能也
。』 (*LJ*, 5b)

Section Nine

The Master said: "It is possible for one to pacify the nations of the world;
it is possible to reject feudal rank and official emolument; it is possible to
tread on a gleaming blade; but the Mean is impossible to attain."

第十章

子路問「強」。子曰：『南方之強
與？北方之強與？抑＜而＞〔爾〕強
與？寬柔以教，不報無道，南方之
強也。君子居之。衽金革，死而不
厭，北方之強也。而強者居之。故
君子和而不流，強哉矯！中立而不
倚，強哉矯！國有道，不變塞焉，
強哉矯！國無道，至死不變，強哉
矯！』 (*LJ*, 6)

Section Ten

{LJ, 6} Master Lu asked about strength. The Master said: "Do you mean the strength of the South or the strength of the North? Or your own [kind of] strength? To be broadminded and gentle in order to teach, and not to retaliate against those who leave the Dao in their dealings, is the strength of the South. The morally noble man takes that way as his constant resort. To sleep wearing armor and weapons and to die without regret is the strength of the North. Those who are aggressive take this way as their constant resort. So the morally noble man is in harmony with others and yet does not flow [along with them; i.e., does not fall into their bad ways]. Oh, how stalwart! He stands in equilibrium and does not become biased to one side or the other. Oh, how stalwart! When the Dao prevails in the nation, he does not change the ways he kept during his earlier obscurity. Oh, how stalwart! When the Dao is abandoned by the nation, he will not change his ways even though it brings about his death. Oh, how stalwart!"

第十一章

子曰：『素隱行怪，後世有述焉，
吾弗爲之矣。君子遵道而行，半
〈塗〉[途] 而廢，吾弗能已矣。君
子依乎中庸，遯世不見知而不悔，
唯聖者能之。』(LJ, 7a)

Section Eleven

{LJ, 7} The Master said: "Some people seek out the hidden and perform marvelous deeds. As a result they become renown in later generations. But I will not do that sort of thing. A nobleman may fare forth on the great

Dao yet give up in mid course. But I can never stop. The morally noble man depends on the Mean, and even though he should achieve no recognition but should [have to] retreat from the world, he would feel no regret. Only the Sage is able to do so."

第十二章

君子之道，費而隱。夫婦之愚，可以與知焉；及其至也，雖聖人亦有所不知焉。夫婦之不肖，可以能行焉；及其至也，雖聖人亦有所不能焉。天地之大也，人猶有所憾。故君子語大，天下莫能載焉；語小，天下莫能破焉。詩云：『鳶飛戾天，魚躍于淵。』言其上下察也。君子之道，造端乎夫婦，及其至也，察乎天地。 (LJ, 7b)

Section Twelve

The Dao of the morally noble man is vast in its application, yet subtle in manifestation. Even the ignorant among common men and women can gain some knowledge of it. But with regard to its utmost reaches, then there are parts regarding which even the Sage remains ignorant. Even the uncouth among the common people can put some of it into operation. But with regard to its utmost reaches, there are some applications that not even the Sage can perform. Despite the grandeur of Heaven and Earth, human beings still find cause for dissatisfaction with them. Thus the words of the Sage [regarding it] are so great that nothing in the world is sufficient to bear them up. His words are so subtle that nothing in the world is able to sunder them. When the *Book of Odes* says: "The hawk flies up to heaven. The fish dives into the abyss,"[2] it speaks of reaching the limits of the world. Just so, the Dao of the morally noble man has its beginning in [the relationship between] man and woman. But at its greatest extension, it exhausts the limits of Heaven and Earth.

第十三章

子曰：『道不遠人，人之爲道而遠人，不可以爲道。詩云：「伐柯，伐柯，其則不遠。」執柯以伐柯，睨而視之，猶以爲遠。故君子以人治人，改而止。忠恕違道不遠，施諸己而不願，亦勿施於人。君子之道四，丘未能一焉。所求乎子以事父，未能也；所求乎臣以事君，未能也；所求乎弟以事兄，未能也；所求乎朋友先施之，未能也。庸德之行，庸言之謹；有所不足，不敢不勉；有餘不敢盡。言顧行，行顧言，君子胡不慥慥爾！』(*LJ*, 8a)

---

2. Mao number 239

Section Thirteen

{*LJ*, 8} The Master said: "The Dao does not make itself remote from people. But when people make [their own] dao, they may make it remote from the human. [So] it is not permissible to make a dao."

[What is the answer then?] The *Book of Odes* says: 'Going to cut an ax handle. Going to cut an ax handle. Its pattern is not far away.'[3] You may hold an ax handle to cut an ax handle, but if you do not look right at it, its pattern may still seem not to be at hand. So the morally noble man takes the human to treat humans, and stops [only] when they have been cured.

By [employing] loyalty and empathy one will deviate little from the Dao. If you are unwilling that something be used on yourself, then do not use it on other people either.

The Dao of the morally noble man has four components, and I am not [fully] capable of a single one: I have never been able to serve my father with what I expect from my sons. I have never been able to serve my superiors with what I expect from my subordinates. I have never been able to serve my elder brothers with what I expect from my younger brothers. I have never been able to serve my friends with what I expect from them.

When the ordinary practice of virtue and the ordinary carefulness of speech prove inadequate, I dare not fail to exert myself to the fullest. And when they are more than adequate, I dare not be self-satisfied.

Words must be tested by [one's] actions, and actions must be compared with [one's] words. Why should the morally noble man not earnestly apply himself?

3. Mao number 158.

第十四章

君子素其位而行，不願乎其外。素
富貴，行乎富貴；素貧賤，行乎貧
賤；素夷狄，行乎夷狄；素患難，
行乎患難。君子無入而不自得焉！

在上位不陵下；在下位不援上，正
己而不求於人，則無怨；上不怨天
，下不尤人，故君子居易以俟命，
小人行險以徼幸。 (LJ, 8) 子曰：『射
有似乎君子，失諸正鵠，反求諸其
身。』 (LJ, 9a)

Section Fourteen

{LJ, 9} The morally noble man simply holds to the performance of the
duties of his station. He does not have aspirations beyond his level. When
he is authentically wealthy and of noble status, he acts in accordance with
that wealth and nobility. When he is authentically poor and humble, he
acts in accordance with that poverty and low status. When he is
authentically a member of a barbarian or savage [culture], he does what is
appropriate to life among barbarians and savages. When he is authentically
in misery and calamity, he acts in accord with his misery and calamity.
There are no conditions under which the morally noble man is not
self-possessed.

When he is in the position of a superior, he does not take advantage of his subordinates. When he is in the position of a subordinate, he does not court favor with his superiors. He keeps himself upright and does not demand things from other people, therefore he experiences no resentment. [Should he fail,] he does not resent Heaven above and does not blame people below. So the morally noble man reposes without striving as he waits for what the mandate of Heaven brings him [as recompense for his actions]. The petty man takes risks in order to seek things that he does not deserve.

The Master said: "The practice of archery bears some resemblance to [the general behavior of] the morally noble man: If one misses the target, one must seek the reason in oneself."

第十五章

君子之道，辟如行遠必自邇，辟如
登高必自卑。詩曰：『妻子好合，
如鼓瑟琴；兄弟既翕，和樂且耽；
宜爾室家，樂爾妻〈帑〉〔孥〕。』
子曰：『父母其順矣乎！』 (LJ, 9b)

Section Fifteen

The Dao of the morally noble man can be exemplified by noting that to travel far one must begin from nearby, or by noting that to climb high one must begin from a low place.[4] The *Book of Odes* says: "The harmony between wife and children is like the playing of lutes and harps. One's older and younger brothers having joined in harmony they are joyful and

4. Note the similarity to the *Lao Zi,* chapter 64.

happy. Make placid your household; make joyful your wife and progeny." [5] The Master said: "Would not one's parents approve of such a state of affairs?"

第十六章

子曰：『鬼神之為德，其盛矣乎！視之而弗見，聽之而弗聞，體物而不可遺。使天下之人，〈齊〉〔齋〕明盛服，以承祭祀，洋洋乎如在其上，如在其左右。詩曰：「神之格思，不可度思，矧可射思。」夫微之顯，誠之不可揜如此夫！』 (*LJ*, 10)

Section Sixteen

{*LJ*, 10} The Master said: "Vast indeed are the powers (*de*) of the spirits (*gui shen*). You may look toward them and yet not see them, listen for them and yet not hear them. They are embodied in things and cannot be lost [*i.e.*, are indispensable]. They cause all the people of the world to fast and purify themselves and clothe themselves with ritual correctness in order that the spirits may receive their sacrifices. Vast and ever-flowing, the spirits seem to be above or to be to one's left or right (*i.e.*, they seem to be all around). The *Book of Odes* says: 'The approach of the spirits cannot be foretold. How dare you be lax!'[6] Now the conspicuousness of the subtle and the unconcealability of the integral is just like this."

5. Mao number 164.
6. Mao number 256.

Commentary:

Here we find *cheng* (integrity) once again. It is the same as in the passage from the sixth section of the *Great Learning*, p. 186, that says "when there is an uncontradicted, integral state within, it must take form externally [in the behavior, non-verbal communications, etc., of the person.]" The spirits are not divided internally or at war with themselves. Therefore they form an irrepressible force in the world.

第十七章

子曰：『舜其大孝也與！德爲聖人，尊爲天子，富有四海之內；宗廟饗之，子孫保之。故大德，必得其位，必得其祿，必得其名，必得其壽。故天之生物，必因其材而篤焉，故栽者培之，傾者覆之。詩曰：「嘉樂君子，憲憲令德，宜民宜人，受祿于天；保佑命之，自天申之」，故大德者必受命。』 *(LJ, 11)*

Section Seventeen

{*LJ*, 11} The Master said: "How magnificent was the filial piety of Shun! With respect to innate virtue, he was a Sage. Due to the respect people felt for him, he was the Son of Heaven. In wealth, he had all within the Four Seas. [In death], he receives sacrifices in the ancestral temple, and his sons and grandsons (*i.e.* descendents) protect him [by assuring the continuation of sacrifices to him]. So a great virtue must receive its due position [in the hierarchy], it must receive its corresponding official emolument, it must receive its corresponding fame, and it must receive its corresponding ripe old age. Thus all of the living things of this world must receive benefaction according to the measure of their talents. So those things which are fit to be planted will be cultivated, and those things which tilt to one side will be overturned. The *Book of Odes* says: 'How good and joyful is the noble man. Overflowing is his beautiful virtue. He benefits the commoners and officials. He receives blessings from Heaven, which aids him and gives him its Mandate to rule. It extends [his rule].' [7] So those who have great virtue must receive their Mandate."

第十八章

子曰：『無憂者，其惟文王乎！以王季爲父，以武王爲子；父作之，子述之。武王纘大王、王季、文王之緒，壹戎衣而有天下，身不失天下之顯名；尊爲天子，富有四海之內；宗廟饗之，子孫保之。武王末受命，周公成文武之德，追王大王、王季，上祀先公以天子之禮。斯禮也，達乎諸侯、大夫及士、庶人。父爲大夫，子爲士；葬以大夫，祭以士。父爲士，子爲大夫，葬以士，祭以大夫。期之喪，達乎大夫

---

7. Mao number 249.

；三年之喪，達乎天子；父母之喪
，無貴賤，一也。」(LJ, 12)

Section Eighteen

{*LJ, 12*} The Master said: "Only King Wen was truly without regrets. King Ji was his father, and King Wu was his son. His father gave rise to his work and his son carried it on for him. King Wu carried on the work of King Tai (his great-grandfather), King Ji, and King Wen. No sooner had he donned armor than he [overcame the then emperor of the Shang and] assumed the throne of the entire world. He did not lose the reputation [that his forebear had acquired] in the world. Due to the respect felt for him, he was the Son of Heaven. His wealth encompassed the entire world. He received sacrifices in the ancestral temples, and his sons and grandsons protected [his sacrifices]. King Wu received the Mandate in his old age. The Duke of Zhou brought the virtuous [accomplishments] of Kings Wen and Wu to completion. He retroactively raised King Tai and King Ji to the status of king. He paid respect to the earlier reigning dukes with the ritual appropriate to the Son of Heaven. This ritual [principle of paying respect to one's ancestors according to one's own rank] was then caused to reach down as far as the several [ranks of] feudal lords, the *dai-fu* (great officers), the knight-scholars [*shi*], and even the common people: If the father is a *dai-fu* and the son is a knight-scholar, then the father is buried according to his status of *dai-fu*, but he receives sacrifices according to the knight-scholar status of the son. If the father was a knight-scholar and the son is a *dai-fu*, then the father is buried according to his status as knight-scholar, but he receives sacrifices according to the *dai-fu* status of the son. The one-year mourning period for all members of the family [except for in-laws] is enjoined on all up to the rank of *dai-fu*. The [requirement for a] three-year mourning [for parents] extends to the Son of Heaven. The mourning for parents is the same for all people regardless of status.

第十九章

子曰：『武王、周公其達孝矣乎！夫孝者善繼人之志，善述人之事者也。春秋，修其祖廟，陳其宗器，設其裳衣，薦其時食。

『宗廟之禮，所以序昭穆也；序爵，所以辨貴賤也；序事，所以辨賢也；旅酬下爲上，所以逮賤也；燕毛，所以序齒也。

『踐其位，行其禮，奏其樂；敬其所尊，愛其所親；事死如事生，事亡如事存，孝之至也。

『郊社之禮，所以事上帝也；宗廟之禮，所以祀乎其先也。明乎郊社之禮，禘嘗之義，治國其如示諸掌乎！』 *(LJ, 13)*

Section Nineteen

{*LJ*, 13} The Master said: "Oh, how perfect was the filial piety of King Wu and the Duke of Zhou. Now one who displays filial piety is good at fulfilling [his father's] aspirations, and skillful at carrying forward the undertakings that [his father] has begun. During the spring and autumn [sacrificial periods one should] make repairs to the ancestral temples, display their [ancestral] sacrificial vessels, exhibit their ceremonial robes, and present the seasonal offerings.

"The ritual of the ancestral temple is that by which sequence is given to the *zhao* and *mu* [alternate lines of royal succession]. Giving proper sequence to feudal ranks is that by which distinctions between nobility and commoners are produced. Giving precedence to deeds and services [in the ancestral temple] is the way that distinction is given to the accomplishments of the worthies. In performing the ceremony of drinking, subordinates serve superiors. Thus a position of dignity is given to the lesser among them. To arrange seating [for ceremonial drinking] according to hair color (*i.e.*, whether or not one has greying hair) is how proper sequence is given according to age.

"Stand in [your ancestor's] position, perform his rituals, play his music, pay respect to those he held in esteem, love those for whom he felt affection, serve the dead as you would serve the living, serve those who have perished as you would serve those who have been preserved — that is the highest degree of filial piety.

"The ceremony [to Heaven and Earth] made at the suburban altar is that by which the Lord on High is served. The ceremony in the ancestral temple is that by which one makes sacrifices to one's ancestors. If one is clear with regard to the ceremonies of the suburban altar, and the responsibilities of the sacrifice made every fifth year to the high ancestors and the other royal ancestral sacrifices, then ruling the country will be [as simple] as looking at one's own palm."

第二十章

哀公問政。子曰：『文、武之政，布在方策。其人存，則其政舉；其人亡，則其政息。人道敏政，地道敏樹。夫政也者，蒲盧也。』故爲政在人；取人以身，修身以道，修道以仁。仁者，人也，親親爲大；義者，宜也，尊賢爲大。親親之殺，尊賢之等，禮所生也。〈在下位，不獲乎上，民不可得而治矣。〉故君子不可以不修身；思修身，不可以不事親；思事親，不可以不知人；思知人，不可以不知天。

天下之達道五，所以行之者三，曰：君臣也，父子也，夫婦也，昆弟也，朋友之交也，五者，天下之達道也；知、仁，勇，三者，天下之達德也；所以行之者，一也。或生而知之，或學而知之，或困而知之

，及其知之，一也。或安而行之，
或利而行之，或勉强而行之，及其
成功，一也。』(LJ, 14)

子曰：『好學近乎知，力行近乎仁
，知恥近乎勇。知斯三者，則知所
以修身；知所以修身，則知所以治
人；知所以治人，則知所以治天下
國家矣。』

凡爲天下國家有九經，曰：修身也
，尊賢也，親親也，敬大臣也，體
群臣也，子庶民也，來百工也，柔
遠人也，懷諸侯也。修身，則道立
；尊賢，則不惑；親親，則諸父昆
弟不怨；敬大臣，則不眩；體群臣
，則士之報禮重；子庶民，則百姓
勸；來百工，則財用足；柔遠人，
則四方歸之；懷諸侯，則天下畏之
。(LJ, 15)

〈齊〉〔齋〕明盛服，非禮不動，所以修身也；去讒遠色，賤貨而貴德，所以勸賢也；尊其位，重其祿，同其好惡，所以勸親親也。官盛任使，所以勸大臣也；忠信重祿，所以勸士也；時使薄斂，所以勸百姓也；日省月試，既廩稱事，所以勸百工也；送往迎來，嘉善而矜不能，所以柔遠人也；繼絕世，舉廢國，治亂持危，朝聘以時，厚往而薄來，所以懷諸侯也。 (LJ, 16)凡爲天下國家有九經，所以行之者，一也。

凡事豫則立，不豫則廢；言前定則不跲，事前定，則不困；行前定，則不疚；道前定，則不窮。 (LJ, 17)

在下位，不獲乎上，民不可得而治矣；獲乎上有道，不信乎朋友，不獲乎上矣；信乎朋友有道，不順乎親，不信乎朋友矣；順乎親有道，

反諸身不誠，不順乎親矣；誠身有
道，不明乎善，不誠乎身矣。(LJ, 18)

誠者，天之道也；誠之者，人之道
也。誠者，不勉而中，不思而得，
從容中道，聖人也；誠之者，擇善
而固執之者也。

博學之，審問之，慎思之，明辨之
，篤行之。有弗學，學之弗能弗措
也；有弗問，問之弗知弗措也；有
弗思，思之弗得弗措也；有弗辨，
辨之弗明弗措也；有弗行，行之弗
篤弗措也。人一能之，己百之；人
十能之，己千之。果能此道矣，雖
愚必明，雖柔必強。(LJ, 19)

Section Twenty

Duke Ai asked about government. The Master said: "The government
[system] of King Wen and King Wu has been displayed on rectangular
writing tablets. When those people were in existence (reigned?), their
governance flourished, but when they perished, their governance was
extinguished. The sensitive part of the processes of human [society] is

governance. The sensitive part of the processes of earth is planting. Governing is like rushes and reeds." Why? Conducting government depends on people [just as growing rushes and reeds depends on an ample supply of water]. People [ought to be] selected according to their character. Character is cultivated according to the dao (way or process that is actually followed), and their dao is cultivated by [the drive called] benevolence. Benevolence (or humanity, *ren* 仁) means human (*ren* 人). And the greatest in that category is to be affectionate to your relatives. The sense of right and wrong (*yi* 義) means 'doing what is appropriate [to the social context]' (*yi* 宜), and, in that category, paying due respect to worthy people is the greatest. The gradations of affection for one's relatives and the levels of respect given to worthy people are what are produced by the sense of ceremony (*li*).[8] So the morally noble man cannot fail to cultivate his character. If one intends to cultivate one's character, then one cannot fail to serve one's relatives. If one intends to serve one's relatives, then one cannot fail to learn about human beings. If one intends to learn about human beings, then one cannot fail to learn about Heaven.

"There are five supreme dao (ways) in the world, and [the means] by which one travels them are three. To wit: [The dao of] interaction between superior and subordinate, father and son, husband and wife, elder and younger brother, and friend and friend. Those five are the five supreme dao. Wisdom, benevolence, and bravery are the highest virtues in the world. That by which they are put into operation is Unity, (*i.e.*, integrity). Whether one is born knowing it, or learns it by study, or learns it through facing adversity, when one at last knows it, it is the same [for all people]. Whether one puts it into effect while remaining entirely at ease, puts it into effect with facility, or puts it into effect only with great difficulty, when success is achieved, it is one and the same."

8. A sentence is omitted here because it is an intrusion from later in this section.

{*LJ*, 15} The Master said: "A love of study is near to wisdom. Vigorous application is near to benevolence. Knowing what is shameful is near to courage. If you know these three, then you know how to cultivate your character. If you know how to cultivate your character, then you know how to govern other people.[9] If you know how to govern other people, then you know how to govern the nations of the world.

"All governance (*wei*) of the countries of the world has nine constant and unvarying elements (*jing*): Cultivating one's own character, honoring worthy people, loving one's relatives, paying respect to the great ministers, being able to put one's self in the position of the multitude of [lesser] ministers, treating the common people as though they were one's own children, assembling the hundred kinds of workers, treating the [visiting] distant peoples gently, and cherishing the nobles [of all countries]. If one's character is cultivated, then the Dao will be established. If one pays respect to worthy people, then one will be kept from making errors of judgment. If one loves one's relatives, then one's elders and one's older and younger brothers will not feel resentment. If one pays respect to the great ministers, then one will not lose one's way [in conducting affairs of state]. If one puts oneself in the position of the multitude of ordinary officials, then they will respond with great deference. If one treats the common people as one's own children, then they will be [easily] swayed by advice. If one assembles the hundred kinds of workers, then there will be enough commodities to supply the needs of the community. If one treats the distant peoples gently, then the people on all four sides will put themselves under one's protection. If one cherishs the nobles [of all countries?], then the whole world will hold one in awe.

{*LJ*, 16} "To fast and purify oneself and clothe oneself with ritual correctness, not daring to do anything that contravenes ritual requirements, is the way to correct one's character.

9. You know what really works, not what might seem to work.

"To get rid of calumny, stay far from sexual encounters, and to value goods lightly but value virtue highly is the way to encourage worthiness [in other people]. To pay deference to their status, increase their emoluments, and sympathize with their likes and dislikes is how to encourage people to be affectionate to their relatives. To let their [subordinate] officials be many in order that they may carry out their duties is the way to encourage the great ministers. To show confidence in them and to pay them well is the way to encourage the knight-scholars. To employ them in accord with the seasons and to tax them lightly is the way to encourage the hundred clans (*i.e.*, the common people). To supervise them daily and to examine them every month, and to reward them with grain in accord with their services, is the way to encourage the hundred classes of artisans. To escort those who are departing, to go out to welcome those who are coming to visit, to laud the good and to commiserate with those of no great ability is the way to be gentle to distant peoples. To restore [noble?] family lines that have been cut off, and to revive countries that have been extinguished, to bring order to the disorderly, to sustain those in danger, to hold court at timely periods, to give them great presents when they depart to their feudal domains after a royal audience but to expect that they bring little as gifts when they come to court is the way to cherish the feudal lords. {*LJ*, 17} There are nine constants in ruling the nations of the world, and that by which they are put into practice is One (unity, integrity).

"In all affairs, with preparation there follows success, and without it, there follows failure. If one's words are prepared beforehand, there will be no slips. If affairs are prepared beforehand, there will be no difficulties. If one's actions are prepared beforehand, then there will be no anguish. If one's dao (course) is prepared beforehand, there will be no dead ends.

{*LJ*, 18} "If one in a lower status cannot gain acceptance by his superiors, then he will be unable to successfully govern the people. There is a dao for gaining acceptance by one's superiors: If one is not trusted by one's friends, one will not be accepted by one's superiors. There is a dao for being trusted by one's friends: If one is not complaisant toward one's parents, one will not be trusted by one's friends. There is a dao for being complaisant toward one's parents: If one introspects on one's own character and discovers a lack of integrity, one will not be complaisant toward one's parents. There is a dao for gaining integrity of character: If one does not have a clear understanding of the good (*i.e.*, that which is to be found in one's *xing*), one will not have integrity of character.

{*LJ*, 19} "Integrity is the dao of Heaven. To integrate [oneself] is the dao of human beings. Those who have integrity effortlessly hit the target, get things without thinking, and self-assuredly come into compliance with the Dao. Such is the Sage. Those who [need to] integrate themselves select the good and hold tightly to it.

"Study [the way to integrity?] in an extensive way, minutely inquire about things, carefully think about things, acutely discriminate them, and wholeheartedly carry them into practice. There may be that which one does not study, but if one should study something then while one is yet unable to do it, one should not put it aside. There may be that into which one does not make inquiry, but if one should inquire into something and yet not know, then one should not put it aside. There may be that about which one does not think, but if one thinks about something and yet does not get it, then one should not put it aside. There may be that which one does not try to discriminate, but if one attempts to discriminate something and does not get clear on it, then one should not put it down. There may be that which one does not undertake, but if one does undertake something and has not yet done it wholeheartedly, one should not put it aside. Other people may be able to do something the first time they try, and you may require one hundred attempts. Other people may be able to do something in ten attempts, and you may require one thousand attempts. But if you are able to use this dao, even though you are stupid, you will become intelligent, and even though you are weak, you will become strong."

Commentary:

The foregoing passage is extremely important as a summation of Confucian ethical theory.

第二十一章

自誠明，謂之性；自明誠，謂之教
。誠則明矣，明則誠矣。 (LJ, 20a)

Section Twenty-one

{*LJ*, 20} The process from integrity (*i.e.*, what is inherently within a person in perfect form) to clear knowledge is ascribed to *xing* (human nature). The process from clear knowledge to integrity is called education. If one has integrity, one will attain clear knowledge; and if one has clear knowledge, one will attain integrity.

Commentary:

This passage is the source of Zhu Xi's doctrine that a kind of gestalt closure occurs in moral learning — one typically begins inquiry in nearly total ignorance and confusion. But gradually one makes some order out of one's seemingly random impressions of the world. Suddenly something "clicks" and a knowledge that is greater than the sum of its parts results. One can acquire such knowledge that goes beyond the evidence that makes up its parts because the structure of the universe is homologous with the structure of the mind. Even though the mind is originally a blank with regard to the particulars of the world, the mind operates according to the same principles that created the universe. Given a large part of a jigsaw puzzle, the mind can both figure out how they go together and also supply some minor missing parts of the puzzle. (See page 185.)

When one has an integral understanding of part of one's world, that is, when one's mind has organized a body of information to make a perfect map of that part of the world, then one is enabled to extrapolate from that map — to gain knowledge about some heretofore unexplored parts of the world. We have the most central parts of the map perfect within us at birth. Those parts are our ethical nature, our *xing*. On the basis of that knowledge alone we can most often tell what we ought to do in response to events having ethical import.[10]

第二十二章

唯天下至誠，爲能盡其性，能盡其
性，則能盡人之性；能盡人之性，
則能盡物之性；能盡物之性，則可
以贊天地之化育，可以贊天地之化
育，則可以與天地參矣 。 (LJ, 20b)

Section Twenty-two

Only the most fully integrated people in the world can fulfill their *xing* (natures). If a person is able to fulfill his own *xing,* then he can fulfill the *xing* of other people. If he is able to fulfill the *xing* of other people, then he can fulfill the *xing* of creatures. If he is able to fulfill the *xing* of creatures, then he can participate in the production-by-transformation of Heaven and Earth. If he can participate in the production-by-transformation of Heaven and Earth, then he can form a trine with Heaven and Earth.

10. See "Learning by Instinct" by James L. Gould and Peter Marler in the January, 1987 issue of *Scientific American,* p. 74ff.

第二十三章

其次致曲，曲能有誠，誠則形，形
則著，著則明，明則動，動則變，
變則化，唯天下至誠爲能化。 *(LJ, 21)*

Section Twenty-three

{*LJ*, 21} Next in order are those who fulfill the imperfect. The imperfect can come to have integrity. With integrity, there comes form (external manifestation?). With form, there comes prominence. With prominence, there comes clarity. With clarity, there comes activity (moving or motivating people?). With activity, there comes change (of the behavior of others?). With change, there comes transformation. It is only the most fully integral in the world who are able to transform [others?].

第二十四章

至誠之道，可以前知；國家將興，
必有禎祥；國家將亡，必有妖孽；
見乎蓍龜，動乎四體；禍福將至，
善，必先知之，不善，必先知之。
故至誠如神。 *(LJ, 22)*

Section Twenty-four

{*LJ*, 22} The process (dao) of greatest integrity is (*i.e.*, implies) the ability to know what is yet to come. When a nation is about to flourish, there must be auspicious omens. When a nation is about to perish, there must be bad omens. They make their appearances in the milfoil [of the *Book of Changes*] and the tortoise shells [used for scapulimancy].[11] Their movements take form in the four limbs. When disaster or good fortune is about to appear those who have integrity must know whether what is to happen is good or bad. So those of the highest integrity are godlike.

第二十五章

誠者，自成也；而道，自道（導）也。誠者，物之終始。不誠，無物。是故，君子誠之為貴。誠者，非自成己而已也，所以成物也。成己，仁也。成物，知也。性之德也，合外內之道也，故時措之宜也。

(*LJ*, 23a)

11. Scapulimancy is divination by reading cracks produced when a heated metal rod is applied to the shoulder blades of sheep or other mammals or the shells of turtles.

Section Twenty-five

{*LJ*, 23} Integrating means to complete oneself. [Going along one's own] dao (functioning autonomously) means to guide oneself. Integrity is the beginning and end of [all] things. If there were no integrity, then there could be nothing. For this reason the morally noble man values integrity highly. Integrating does not mean completing oneself alone; it is also that by which all things are completed. To be able to complete oneself (ones own kind) is [a direct result of] benevolence. To be able to complete other things is [a result of] knowledge or wisdom. [These two] are the powers (*de*) pertaining to the *xing* (nature of a human being). By [this nature] the Dao of the external [universe] is united with the dao of the internal (*i.e.*, the microcosm within each human being). Therefore it is appropriate to all circumstances.

Commentary:

This passage is expecially important in helping to define *cheng* because it shows that to *cheng* some one means to engage in a process of growth and completion.

N.B. Here we have the process of integration extending beyond the individual to the entire universe.

第二十六章

故至誠無息；不息則久。久則徵，徵則悠遠，悠遠則博厚，博厚則高明。博厚所以載物也；高明所以覆物也，悠久所以成物也。博厚配地，高明配天，悠久無疆。如此者，不見而章，不動而變，無爲而成。

天地之道，可一言而盡也：『其為
物不貳，則其生物不測。』天地之
道：博也，厚也，高也，明也，悠
也，久也。 *(LJ, 23b)* 今夫天，斯昭昭
之多，及其無窮也，日月星辰繫焉
，萬物覆焉。今夫地，一撮土之多
；及其廣厚，載華嶽而不重，振河
海而不洩，萬物載焉。今夫山，一
卷石之多，及其廣大，草木生之，
禽獸居之，寶藏興焉。今夫水，一
勺之多，及其不測，黿鼉蛟龍魚鱉
生焉，貨財殖焉。

詩云：『維天之命，於穆不已。』
蓋曰天之所以為天也。『於乎不顯
，文王之德之純。』蓋曰文王之所
以為文也，純亦不已。 *(LJ, 24)*

Section Twenty-six

So the most completely integrated [virtue of a person?] suffers no internal discontinuities; since it suffers no discontinuities, it is long-enduring. Since it is long-enduring, [its goodness, its integrity] is manifested externally. Since it is manifested externally, it acts at a great distance. Since it acts at a great distance, it becomes widespread and substantial. Since it is widespread and substantial, it becomes high and clear. Because it is widespread and substantial, it can bear up creatures. Since it is high and clear, it can cover over those creatures. Because it acts at a great distance and is long-enduring, it [engenders and] brings the creatures [of the world] to completion. Because it is widespread and substantial, it is a match for Earth. Because it is high and clear, it is a match for Heaven. Because it acts at a distance and is long-enduring, it is boundless. In the case of a thing such as this, even though it is not visible it is yet readily apparent. Although it does not move, it [produces] changes. Although it does not do anything, it yet brings things to completion.[12]

The dao of Heaven and Earth can be fully expressed in one saying: "As a thing it is characterized as being without duplicity (lit., two), so its production of creatures is unfathomable." The Dao of Heaven and Earth is broad and substantial, high and bright, far-reaching and long enduring. {LJ, 24} Now with regard to heaven (the sky), it [starts with] no more than a patch of brightness, but when it is viewed in its infinite extent, [even] the sun, moon, and stars are attached to it, and the myriad creatures are covered by it. Now with regard to the earth, it [starts with] no more than a pinch of dirt, but when it is regarded in [its full] breadth and thickness, it is seen to bear up Mount Hua and Mount Yue without counting them as heavy, it receives the rivers and seas and does not void them somewhere else, it bears up the myriad creatures. Now with regard to the mountains, they [start with] a fist-sized piece of rock; when they are contemplated in [their full] breadth and greatness, grass and trees grow from them, birds and beasts dwell on them, and stores full of precious things arise therein. Now with regard to water, it [starts with] a mere spoonful, but when we extend our view to its fathomlessness, sea monsters, flood dragons, fish, and turtles are produced therein and precious resources are concentrated therein.

12. Note the very Daoist feeling of some of these pronouncements.

The *Book of Odes* says: "The mandate of Heaven is profound and infinite."[13] This must refer to the reason that Heaven can be Heaven (*i.e.*, act as Heaven does). The *Book of Odes* says: "Is it not indeed brilliant, the purity of the virtue of King Wen!"[14] This must mean that the reason that King Wen could be King Wen (*i.e.*, the reason he could be such a good king) was that he was pure and unbounded.

第二十七章

大哉！聖人之道！洋洋乎，發育萬物，峻極於天。優優大哉！禮儀三百，威儀三千，待其人｜然｜｜而｜後行。故曰：『苟不至德，至道不凝焉』。 *(LJ, 25)* 故君子尊德性而道問學，致廣大而盡精微，極高明而道終庸。溫故而知新，敦厚以崇禮。 *(LJ, 26)* 是故，居上不驕，為下不倍。國有道，其言足以興；國無道，其默足以容。詩曰：『既明且哲，以保其身』，其此之謂與。 *(LJ, 27)*

13. Mao number 267.
14. Mao number 260.

Section Twenty-seven

{*LJ*, 25} How great is the Dao of the Sage! Vast, it produces and nurtures the myriad creatures. In its height and magnitude, it reaches to Heaven. How abundant in their greatness are the three hundred major ceremonies and three thousand minor ceremonies [of the Zhou dynasty]; all must await the proper person to be [concretely, efficaciously] performed. So it is said: "If it (one's nature) is not one having the highest virtue, the great Dao will not accumulate therein." {*LJ*, 26} Therefore, the morally noble man reverently serves [his own] virtuous nature (*de xing*) and takes inquiry and study as his dao. He carries his studies into the broadest reaches and approaches the limits of the most subtle and minute. He goes to the highest eminence [of intelligence] and [yet] takes the Mean as his dao. He reviews the old in order to know the new. He is sincere and wholehearted in order to pay full respects to the rites. {*LJ*, 27} For this reason, when he holds a high position, he is not haughty, and when he holds a lowly position, he does not become insubordinate. When the state is governed according to the dao, his words are sufficient to cause him to prevail. When the state is not governed according to the dao, his silence is sufficient to absorb and contain (*i.e.*, he does not react to provocations in such a way as to make things worse). That must be what the *Book of Odes* means when it says: "He is both bright and wise and so is able to protect his character."[15]

第二十八章

子曰：『愚而好自用；賤而好自專；生乎今之世，反古之道；如此者，災及其身者也。』

15. Mao number 260.

非天子不議禮，不制度，不考文。
今天下，車同軌，書同文，行同倫
。雖有其位，苟無其德，不敢作禮
樂焉；雖有其德，苟無其位，亦不
敢作禮樂焉 ○ (LJ, 28)

子曰：『吾說夏禮，杞不足徵也；
吾學殷禮，有宋存焉；吾學周禮，
今用之，吾從周 ○ 』 (LJ, 29a)

Section Twenty-eight

{LJ, 28} The Master said: "Stupid and yet desirous of doing things his own way; ignoble and yet desirous of taking himself as sole authority; born in today's world, yet reverting to the dao [that has come down to us] from antiquity — People like this will bring calamity on themselves."

One who is not a Son of Heaven (*i.e.*, king or emperor) should not discourse on the rituals, should not establish ordinances, should not authenticate the forms of Chinese characters. In the world of today, the carts make ruts of the same width, people all write the same Chinese characters, and behavior is all judged by the same ethical standards. Even though someone may hold a certain position in society, if he does not have a commensurate virtue, then he dares not institute rituals and dares

not compose music.[16] Even though a person may have the requisite virtue,
·should he not hold the appropriate position in society, he will not dare to
make rites and music.

{*LJ*, 29} The Master said: "What I say about the rites of the Xia dynasty
cannot be attested by Qi (its successor state). When I study the rituals of
the Yin (*i.e.*, Shang) dynasty, there is yet [the successor state of] Song [to
give evidence concerning their ancestors' practices]. When I study the
rituals of the Zhou dynasty, since they are in use at present, I will follow
their prescriptions."

Commentary:

Although this passage seems to tell of events occuring during the Zhou dynasty, I
believe that it is actually intended to discuss what should be the proper attitude of
educated people at a time when the Zhou is either on the verge of collapse or has
already collapsed. In its mention of the various activities of standardization, it
seems to reflect conditions during or after the Qin dynasty, but since this document
supports humanistic Confucianism rather than the totalitarian doctrines behind the
Qin rule, called Legalism, it would hardly seem to stand as a rationalization for the
immediate successor state to the Zhou. On the other hand, it supports the sole right
of the throne to set these various standards. So I think the text, or at least this part
of the text, may have been written during the early Han dynasty to support the idea
of Confucian rule.

16. Rather than composing music, this passage may actually refer to determining
the exact pitches of the base notes used for forming the various Chinese scales.

第二十九章

王天下有三重焉，其寡過矣乎！上焉者，雖善無徵，無徵不信，不信民弗從。下焉者，雖善不尊，不尊不信，不信民弗從。故君子之道，本諸身，徵諸庶民，考諸三王而不繆，建諸天地而不悖，質諸鬼神而無疑，百世以俟聖人而不惑。質諸鬼神而無疑，知天也；百世以俟聖人而不惑，知人也。是故，君子動而世為天下道，行而世為天下法，言而世為天下則；遠之則有望，近之則不厭。詩曰：『在彼無惡，在此無射；庶幾夙夜，以永終譽』。君子未有不如此，而〈蚤〉〔早〕有譽於天下者也。 (LJ, 29)

Section Twenty-nine

There have been three (levels =) eras in ruling the world; [knowing about them] can indeed minimize errors.[17]

In the case of those above/superior/prior thereto, although they are good there is no evidence, and since there is no evidence they cannot be believed, and since they cannot be believed, the people would not follow them.[18]

In the case of those below/inferior/posterior thereto, although they are good they have no position of [automatic] respect, since they have no position of [automatic] respect they are not believed in, and since they are not believed in, the people will not follow them.[19]

So the dao of the morally noble man is based on character, is evidenced in the multitudes, and is tested by the institutions of the three ancient dynasties and shown to be without error. It can then be established in the world between Heaven and Earth and create therein no conflict; it can be questioned before the ghosts and spirits and no doubt be found concerning it. Though the world should wait a hundred generations for another Sage [who could then evaluate it], it would not come into doubt in the interim. It may be questioned before the ghosts and spirits and no doubt be found concerning it because he knows Heaven. It can wait for a hundred generations for another Sage and not come into doubt because he knows humans. For this reason, when the morally noble man moves, the people

17. This sentence may possibly refer to the pre-Zhou, Zhou, and post-Zhou eras.
18. This sentence seems to refer to the dynasties prior to the Zhou and to their institutions.
19. This passage seems to refer to various possible successor houses to the Zhou.

of that generation take what he does to be the dao of the world. When he acts, the generation takes it to be the law of the world. When he speaks, the generation takes it to be the pattern of the world. At a distance, people see someone to look up to, and close at hand they do not find him oppressive. The *Book of Odes* says: "Over there, there is nothing to detest. On this side, there is nothing to dislike. By day and by night, seemingly without any interruption, the people give praise forever."[20] In the case of morally noble men, there are none who are exceptions to this [testing and validation] and are yet soon renowned throughout the world.

第三十章

仲尼祖述堯舜，憲章文武；上律天
時，下襲水土。辟如天地之無不持
載，無不覆幬；辟如四時之錯行，
如日月之代明。萬物並育而不相害
，道並行而不相悖。小德川流，大
德敦化。此天地之所以爲大也。

(LJ, 30a)

20. Mao number 278.

Section Thirty

{*LJ*, 30} Zhong-ni (*i.e.*, Confucius) passed down the tradition and teachings of Yao and Shun. He modeled himself on and glorified King Wen and King Wu. He emulated the seasons of the heavens above and conformed himself to the waters and lands below. He was like Heaven and Earth in the way that there was nothing that they did not support and bear up and envelop and cover. He was like the four seasons in the way that each links to the succeeding season, and like the sun and the moon in the manner that they alternate at making brightness. [So] he was like the myriad creatures in the way that they all develop together and [their mutual development] does no injury to others; and like the [various] dao [in the world] that move side by side and do not conflict with each other; the lesser powers (*de*, "virtues") flow and eventually merge without ever working at cross-purposes; the greater virtues transform and thereby deepen and magnify. The above [capabilities] are the very reason that are Heaven and Earth able to be great.

第三十一章

唯天下至聖，為能聰明睿知。足以
有臨也；寬裕溫柔，足以有容也；
發強剛毅，足以有執也；〈齊〉〔齋
〕莊中正，足以有敬也；文理密察
，足以有別也。溥博淵泉，而時出
之。溥博如天，淵泉如淵。見而民
莫不敬，言而民莫不信，行而民莫
不〈説〉〔悅〕。是以聲名洋溢乎中

國，施及蠻貊，舟車所至，人力所
通，天之所覆，地之所載，日月所
照，霜露所隊，凡有血氣者，莫不
尊親，故曰配天。 *(LJ, 30b)*

Section Thirty-one

Only the most sagely of men in the world can be intelligent, enlightened, sagacious, and wise so that they are adequate to supervise others from a position of authority, [can be truly] tolerant, lenient, warm, and flexible so that they are adequate to be accepting of other people; [can truly] take the initiative, be strong, tough, and resolute so that they are adequate to control [others]; [can be truly] chaste, august, unbiased, and upright so that they are adequate to inspire the respect [of the people]; [can be truly] cultured, well-organized, close in their reasoning, and perspicacious so that they are adequate to exercise discrimination.

[These five virtues of the Sages are] vast and ever-reaching, deep, and a ceaseless source; at timely intervals [the virtues] make an appearance. Vast like Heaven, a deep and bottomless source like the abyss, when they appear, none from among the people dare not to be respectful, when they speak, none fail to believe, and when they act, none fail to be pleased. For the foregoing reasons, their reputations are very well known throughout the country and even reach to the barbarians on the periphery. Wherever boats and vehicles can go, wherever human power can reach, in all that is covered by Heaven and all that is sustained by Earth, in all that the sun and the moon shine down upon, and whatever the frost and dew cover, no [creatures] that have blood and breath fail to honor and hold affection [for the Sages]. Therefore, it is said that they are a match for Heaven.

第三十二章

唯天下至誠，爲能經綸天下之大經，立天下之大本，知天地之化育。夫焉有所倚？肫肫其仁，淵淵其淵，浩浩其天。苟不固聰明聖知達天德者，其孰能知之？ *(LJ, 30c)*

Section Thirty-two

Only the most thoroughly integrated people in the world are able to set the great constant [relationships] of the world to rights, to establish the great basis [for moral action] in the world, and to know the production-by-transformation performed by Heaven and Earth. On what else could they depend? How wholesome is benevolence! How deep the abyss! How floodlike is [the power of] Heaven! If they were not indeed acute of perception and did not have sagely wisdom, being men who had attained the very virtues of Heaven, then how could they know of these things?

第三十三章

詩曰：『衣錦尚絅，』惡其文之著也。故君子之道，闇然而日章；小人之道，的然而日亡。君子之道，淡而不厭，簡而文，溫而理；知遠

之近，知風之自，知微之顯，可與
入德矣。

詩云：『潛雖伏矣；亦孔之昭。』
故君子內省不疚，無惡於志。君子
之所不可及者，其唯人之所不見乎
！

詩云：『相在爾室，尚不愧于屋漏
。』故君子不動而敬，不言而信。

詩曰：『奏假無言，時靡有爭。』
是故君子不賞而民勸，不怒而民威
於鈇鉞。

詩曰：『不顯惟德，百辟其刑之。
』是故君子篤恭而天下平。

詩云：『予懷明德，不大聲以色。
』 (LJ, 30d)

子曰：『聲色之於以化民，末也。
』詩曰：『德輶如毛。』毛猶有倫
。『上天之載，無聲無臭。』至矣

O *(LJ, 31)*

Section Thirty-three

The *Book of Odes* says: "She wears a single-layer garment over her brocaded coat."[21] This line indicates that she disliked the opulence of the coat's ornamentation. So the dao of the morally noble man is subdued and yet daily becomes more readily apparent. The dao of the petty man is ostentatious and yet daily becomes more debilitated. The dao of the morally noble man is bland and yet does not oppress, it is simple yet elegant, warm and yet orderly. If one knows the nearness of what is far, if one knows the source of the wind (*i.e.*, phenomena), if one knows the obviousness of what is minute, then one may be admitted to the ranks of the virtuous.

The *Book of Odes* says: "Although [the fish] dives to rest on the bottom of the pool, it is yet clearly (illuminated =) visible."[22] So the morally noble man [only requires that he may] examine himself and find no cause for regret, nor find anything contemptible in his aspirations. The excellence of the morally noble man lies precisely in what is not available to inspection by other people.

21. Mao number 57.
22. Mao number 192.

The *Book of Odes* says [of the morally noble man]: "Behold you in your dwelling; there is no cause for shame even when you are in your innermost chamber."[23] So even though the morally noble man takes no action, he is respected, and although he says nothing, he is believed.

The *Book of Odes* says: "Although [the spirits] enter soundlessly, at that time they cause there to be no contention."[24] Similarly, the morally noble man does not give rewards and yet the people are persuaded; he does not resort to anger and yet the people are more awed than they are by the executioner's ax.

The *Book of Odes* says: "He does not display his virtue and yet the princes follow him."[25] For this reason, the morally noble man is wholeheartedly respectful in attitude and so the world is made tranquil.

The *Book of Odes* says: "I cherish bright virtue, and do not make loud my voice or exaggerate my countenance."[26] {*LJ*, 31} The Master said: "Using the volume of one's voice or the severity of one's countenance to attempt to reform the people is the lowest technique."

The *Book of Odes* says: "His (?) virtue rests [on the people] as lightly as a feather."[27] Even though they be light as feathers, virtues still can be differentiated according to moral worth.

[The *Book of Odes* says:] "The productive activities of Heaven are soundless and odorless."[28] That is the highest [form of transformation].

23. Mao number 256.
24. Mao number 302.
25. Mao number 269.
26. Mao number 241.
27. Mao number 260.
28. Mao number 235.

APPENDIX ONE

Appendix One

This Appendix is intended to demonstrate how the first chapter of the *Lao Zi* is written in parallel passages that show the dichotomy between the hidden and manifest aspects of reality and then asserts that this dichotomy is resolved in a state that involves no opposites and is utterly beyond human awareness. The words *dao* 道 (Way) and *miao* 妙 (ineffable efficacy) obviously describe hidden aspects of reality. The word *shi* 始 (beginning) also indicates a hidden aspect, as is established in the last section of this Appendix. I have set these words, and their English equivalents, in special type faces to suggest the impressions these words might have made on students of the *Lao Zi* at or near the time it was written.

In the following Chinese text, a comma (，) indicates the punctuation I prefer, and a Chinese list-element comma (、) indicates the alternative punctuation. English letters indicate rhymes, and the words 潛, 顯, and 形上 indicate the hidden, manifest, and transcendent aspects of reality respectively. After each line I indicate the reasons for my choice of punctuation.

道：可道，非常道；（潛）   After Song Chang-xing.

名：可名，非常名。0*（顯）   After Song Chang-xing.

無、名，天地之始；A*（潛）   Prefer 2/4 in keeping with next lines.

有、名，萬物之母。A*（顯）   Prefer 2/4 in keeping with next lines.

故

常無、欲，以觀其妙；B*（潛）Prefer 3/4 punctuation. (Meaning)

常有、欲，以觀其徼。B*（顯）Prefer 3/4 punctuation. (Meaning)

此兩者，同、出而異名，O* Prefer 3/5 punctuation. (Balance)

同謂之玄。C*   （形上）   4 syllables only choice.

玄之又玄，眾妙之門。C*（形上）   4 & 4 syllables only choice.

* rhymes

First Interpretation:

Dao: If one can be directed along it, it is not the constant *Dao*.

Name: If one can be given, it is not the constant **Name**.

Nameless is the beginning of Heaven and Earth.

Named is the **mother** of the myriad creatures.

So,

It is always by desirelessness that one sees the hidden (noumenal) aspect,

and always by being in a state of having desires that one observes the **outer** (phenomenal) aspect.

These two [aspects] emerge together and are differently named.

Together they are called the dark and mysterious.

The most dark and mysterious of the dark and mysterious

Is the portal of the multitudinous wonders.

Second Interpretation:

A way (*dao*) that one can be directed along is not the constant Dao.

A name that can be given is not a constant **name**.

"Non-existence" names the beginning of Heaven and Earth.

"Existence" names the **mother** of the myriad creatures.

So,

It is always by desirelessness that one sees the hidden (noumenal) aspect,

and always by being in a state of having desires that one observes the **outer** (phenomenal) aspect.

These two [aspects] emerge together and are differently named.

Together, they are called the dark and mysterious.

The most dark and mysterious of the dark and mysterious

Is the portal of the multitudinous wonders.

Commentary:

Some authorities maintain that lines six and seven above should be interpreted according to the alternative punctuation indicated. If that punctuation is chosen the lines become: "Constant nothingness: [One may] desire to observe its mysteries. Constant being: [One may] desire to observe its outer aspect." (For instance, John C. H. Wu's loose translation of these two lines seems to take this approach even though his punctuation of the Chinese text is the one I prefer.) But not only is the meaning strange, the grammar of the passage also becomes problematical.

Other translators and commentators have not seen the strict alternation (indicated by different type faces in the text above) affirmed to exist between the hidden and manifest (internal and external) aspects of reality. The Dao, understood as the total process of the universe, the *way* things work, is clearly beyond our immediate apprehension. Names, on the other hand, are given to things on the basis of their perceptible differences. The Chinese word for "beginning" is, as I will demonstrate in the second appendix, a cognate for "fœtus," and the word for "mother" is a drawing of the breasts and nipples. Obviously, one is inner and hidden, and the other is outer and manifest. The very essence of something that is *miao* is that it is the hidden aspect of reality that is mysteriously capable of producing wonderful phenomena in the world. It is what some cultures call *manna*. In my notes above, I define it as the "inexplicable efficacies" of the world. To these "inexplicable efficacies" are contrasted the "outer fringes," the outer, phenomenal, aspects of things.

In their transcendent source, which is not perceptible to us, the internal and external aspects of all beings in our universe are collapsed into one. This "One" we can only describe as the "dark and mysterious." This "dark and mysterious" precursor to phenomenal existence is the source of all the multitudes of wonderfully mysterious things in the world. Because this "dark and mysterious" entity is sometimes also called Dao, we see foreshadowed here the frequent confusion in Chinese philosophy between the merely invisible or incomprehensible aspects of this universe and the totally unexperienceable, transcendent, source of this universe. According to this passage, the "dark and mysterious" is logically prior to the Dao that is the total process of the phenomenal universe. So, properly speaking, people should refrain from calling the "dark and mysterious" aspect behind all being the Dao so as to avoid unnecessary confusion.

In the text, the internal and external aspects of the world are discussed on several levels.

The general parallelism of the text is enough to establish that the "beginning" is something that is not open to casual inspection. It has to be the opposite of the clearly visible enlarged breasts and nipples of the mother. But investigation of the structure and history of the Chinese character *shi* 始 gives independent verification of this idea. It seems that at the earliest time the word fœtus was used much as we use the word "seed" to indicate the "source, origin, or beginning" of things. (*New World Dictionary of the American Language*)

APPENDIX TWO

Meaning of the character *shi* 始 in the first chapter of the *Lao Zi*.

The following discussion is based on observations that I had already made before I discovered that the silk texts of the *Lao Zi* simply write *shi* 始 (beginning) as *tai* 台. It would appear that to the scribes who produced the silk texts, the latter was functionally equivalent to the former. But it could also be argued that the correct way to make the meaning of the character more specific would have been to write it as *tai* 胎 (fœtus) instead of *shi* 始 (beginning).

At present there are several words in use in the Chinese that appear to me to be cognates of *shi* 始 even though their current meanings are different, and their pronunciations are also different. Those characters are: *si* 厶, *yi* 以, *tai* 台, *tai* 胎. The first thing to notice is that all these characters include an element that looks like 厶.

According to Bernard Karlgren (*Grammata Serica Recensa*, 557a), the ancient pronunciation of 厶 was *siêr*. He glosses it as meaning "egoistic," and sees it as being later transformed into 私 by the addition of a second element. In modern Chinese, both of these characters are pronounced *si*, and mean the same thing.

Karlgren gives the ancient pronunciation of 以 (to take something to do something else) as *ziêg*. Its oracle bone form is nearly identical to that of *si* 厶. Moreover, the bronze form of *si* is still seen in the "pedantic" form of *yi* 以, which is 㠯. Lin Yi-guang, quoted in Gao Shu-fan's etymological dictionary, says that *yi* is the original form of the character *shi* 始 (to begin, ancient pronunciation *siêg*). Li Jing-zhai, quoted in the same dictionary, argues that *si* 厶 was borrowed to write *yi* 以, and then later *si* was enlarged to 私 to prevent confusion.

If these scholars are both correct, then 厶 gave rise to 以 which gave rise to 始.

The character *si* 厶 is defined in the *Han Fei Zi* as self-proprietorship (of some enterprise). But it is not clear how *yi* comes to mean "to take; to use; in order to; because, etc." The explanation offered in Gao's book, based on Xu Shen's *Shuo Wen Jie Zi*, seems forced.

The ancient pronunciations reconstructed by Karlgren do make it seem that these three words may have had some relation in the spoken language. Perhaps they were cognates. *Si* was pronounced siêr, *shi* was pronounced *siêg*, and *yi* was pronounced *ziêg*. The pronunciation of each of the supposed derivitive characters differs by either an initial consonant or a final consonant.

The two characters for which I assert a cognate relationship pertinent to the first chapter of the *Lao Zi* are *shi* 始 and *tai* 胎. They both share the element now pronounced *tai* 台. Karlgren reconstructs the ancient pronunciation of *tai* as *diêg*, which seems to put it in the same group of sounds in the spoken language. Moreover, *tai* 台 was a loanword for *tai* 鮐, and the latter was pronounced *t'êg*. *T'êg* is also the ancient pronunciation for *tai* 胎. If *t'êg* 鮐 (globefish) could be written *t'êg* 台 then it would seem that *t'êg* 胎 (fœtus) might have been written *t'êg* 台 before a special character for "fœtus" developed. Unfortunately, there does not seem to be an extant instance of the character for fœtus in bronze script. What we do find is 台 used in the silk texts of the *Lao Zi* in a passage where the traditional explanation says that it must mean "to begin." But the pronunciation would suggest that it should mean "fœtus." Of course the reader has probably already guessed that I mean to assert that a fœtus is a prototypical kind of beginning.

The bronze form of the word *zi* 子 (�子) depicts an infant by drawing a proportionately large head on a body of which the arms but not the individual legs are visible. The drawing is similar to the depiction of the character Sweetpea in the Popeye comic strip. We can imagine the legs of the infant depicted in the Chinese character as perhaps being bound in swaddling cloth.

The oracle bone form of the word *si* 厶 (𠫔) seems to show an infant, but the arms have not been drawn. Moreover, the infant is inverted. So in keeping with the meaning of *tai* 胎 it may represent a fœtus awaiting birth. In both *tai* 台 and *tai* 胎 there is a figure below the *si* element that usually means "mouth." But *kou* 口 can mean the mouth of a river, the mouth of a bottle, and so forth. In this case it would appear to represent the entrance to the birth canal. So *tai* 台 would seem to be a drawing of a fœtus poised over the birth canal. *Tai* 胎 merely amplifies that meaning by adding the flesh radical at the left side. *Shi* 始 does the same thing by adding the female radical at the left side.

From the standpoint of ancient pronunciations, the relationship postulated here seems plausible. From left to right in the chart on the next page, the ancient pronunciations are siêr, ziêg, diêg, t'êg, and síêg. Note that all the initial consonants are made in approximately the same position in the mouth. Similarly, the final r and final g are made in approximately the same position in the mouth.

From the standpoint of the original meanings of these character, once it be postulated that 厶 depicts a fœtus, it is fairly easy to see how all of these characters might be related as cognates.

Si (厶 or modern 私) means "private, personal, selfish, etc.," and *tai* 台 means "I, me," so the connection between these two words is fairly direct. Similarly, the connection between *tai* 胎 and shi 始 is straightforward.

The idea of fœtus is probably related to the idea of personhood by the fact that the fœtus is the earliest stage of anyone's existence. The mental connnection formed is also consonant with the age-old Chinese tendency to refer to oneself in humble terms, to stress one's insignificance. (The Duke of Zhou refers to himself as "the little one" in his petition to the ancestors on high given in the *Brass-bound Coffer*.)

Finally, the fœtus is the basis for development of the mature organism, so if there is indeed a connection between *yi* 以 and the other words in this series it is probably that *yi* originally meant something like "to serve as a basis for," and only later came to mean "take (something) as a basis for doing something else."

sier	*zieg*	*dieg*	*t'eg*	*síeg*	
[graph]	[graph]	(null)	(null)	[graph]	Before 1000 B.C.
Karlgren: ≅*yi*. "Explanation of graph unknown."	=*si* 私 in *HFZ*. Lin Yi-guang: "Original character for *shi*.			Upperright element uncertain.	
[graph]	[graph]	[graph]	[graph]	[graph]	500 B.C.
Form still seen in the "pedantic" form of *yi*, 弖.		= "I," "me" in *Shi Jing* = "to delight" in *Shi Ji* = 悦. Loan for "globefish" *t'eg* 鲐 .	*t'eg*	*sieg*	
[graph]	[graph]	[graph]	[graph]	[graph]	100 A.D.
[graph]	[graph]	[graph]	[graph]	[graph]	Present
si personal, biased toward self, egotistic.	*yi* take, use; in order to; because.	*tai* I, me.	*tai* fœtus.	*shi* beginning; begin; first, as soon as.	

SOME HINTS ON PRONUNCIATION

Some Hints on Pronunciation

Ai sounds like the diphthong English-speakers make in naming the letter "i."

Ben rhymes with "fun."

Bi sounds like "bee."

Bo is difficult to pronounce in English because the "o" is not a diphthong. It is fairly close to the "o" in "porridge."

Chang rhymes with "ping-**pong**."

Cheng sounds like the Chinese surname that is sometimes spelled "Chung" in the United States.

Chu sounds like "choo," but with the tongue held farther back in the mouth so that there is no "w" at the end of the sound.

Cuo sounds like "tswo" and is made with an explosive puffing of air.

Da rhymes with "ma" and "pa."

Dao is pronounced like the "dow" in "dowager."

De sounds like the "duh" sound comic book characters make at time of stupified astonishment.

Di sounds like "dee."

Dian is pronounced like the "dien" in "Dien Bien Phu."

Ding rhymes with "sing."

Duan rhymes with "fawn."

Dui has a vowel sound like the "ai" of "quail."

Dun sounds as if it ought to be written "dwun." The vowel is like the "oo" in "hook."

Fan rhymes with "Kahn."

Fei sounds like "Faye."

Feng rhymes with "sung."

Gao rhymes with "scow."

Gong rhymes with the German surname "Jung."

Guang rhymes with "ping-pong."

Han rhymes with "Kahn."

He sounds like "huh."

Heng rhymes with "stung."

Hu sounds like the way American speakers of English pronounce "who."

Huang rhymes with "ping-pong."

Huai sounds like the way our teachers told us to pronounce "why," i.e., with a strong opening "h" sound.

Hui starts with another "h" sound like those above. It rhymes with "bay."

Ji sounds like "gee," except that the "j" sound is **not** the "zh" sound favored by many radio and television announcers. There is a definite stoppage of breath at the beginning of the word, just as there are in English words that begin with "j." The difference, which people who are not studying the Chinese language may safely ignore, is that the sound is made by placing the surface of the tongue against the top of the mouth rather than by placing the tip of the tongue there.

Jia uses the "j" sound described above, followed by a long "e" sound, followed by an open "a" sound. It rhymes with "Mia," but is one syllable.

Jiang rhymes with "ping-pong." The "j" sound is as described above.

Jing rhymes with "ping." The "j" sound is **not** the "zh" sound favored by many radio and television announcers. There is a definite stoppage of breath at the beginning of the word, just as there are in English words that begin with "j." The difference, which people who are not studying the Chinese language may safely ignore, is that the sound is made by placing the surface of the tongue against the top of the mouth rather than by placing the tip of the tongue there.

Jian is one syllable, with the "j" sound made as described above. The "ian" sound is like the "ien" in "Dien Bien Phu."

Jiao uses the "j" sound described above and rhymes with "meow." It is a one-syllable word.

Jie uses the "j" sound described above, followed by a long "e" sound, followed by the odd sound with which Bugs Bunny announces his presence when he says: "Eh, what's up Doc?" It is a one-syllable word.

Jue uses the "j" sound described above, followed by "ü," followed by the Bugs Bunny "eh" sound.

Ke sounds like "kuh."

Kong rhymes with the German surname "Jung."

Kuang rhymes with "ping-pong."

Lao rhymes with "cow."

Li sounds just like the English surname "Lee."

Ling rhymes with "sing."

Lun has a vowel sound like the "oo" in "cook."

Ma sounds like "ma" or like the "mo" in "moderation."

Mao rhymes with "cow."

Miao sounds like "meow," except that it is all one syllable.

Nan rhymes with "Kahn."

Pan rhymes with "Kahn."

Pen rhymes with "fun."

Pu sounds like "poo."

Qi sounds like "chee," except that the "ch" sound is made with the surface of the tongue as with the "j" sounds above.

Qian uses the "q" or "ch" sound described above. It rhymes with "yen."

Qin sounds like "chin," except that the "ch" sound is made with the surface of the tongue as with the "j" sounds above.

Qing uses the "q" sound described above. It rhymes with "sing."

Qiu sounds like "chyu" and rhymes with "bow."

Ren sounds like the word "wren," except that when properly made the tongue is held very far back in the mouth as when making the "sh" sounds mentioned below.

Shang rhymes with "ping-pong." The "sh" sound is made with the tongue very far back in the mouth. If you get the "ang" to come out all right, then the "sh" will probably be good too.

Shen begins with the "sh" sound described above. It rhymes with "fun."

Sheng begins with the "sh" sound described above. It rhymes with "stung."

Shi has the same "sh" sound found in "shang," but the "i" is pronounced as though it were an "r." So "shi" is like the "sher" of sherbet.

Shu is pronounced rather like the English word "shoe," except that the "sh" sound is made with the tongue very far back in the mouth. If you just say "shoe," Chinese people will probably find that a satisfactory approximation.

Shun uses the "sh" sound described above. It sounds as if it ought to be written "shwun." The vowel is like the "oo" in "hook."

Shuo uses the "sh" sound described above. The "uo" is like the "wa" of the word "walk."

3Si sounds rather like the hissing sound people make at umpires. A little vowel sound comes out at the end as the tip of the tongue is relaxed.

Tai sounds like "tie."

Tang rhymes with "ping-pong."

Wang rhymes with "ping-pong."

Wen sounds like "one."

Wu sounds like "woo."

Xi sounds like "she," except that like the "j" and "q" sounds, the "x" sound is made with the surface rather than with the tip of the tongue.

Xia uses the "x" sound described above, followed by a long "e," followed by an open "a." It rhymes with "Mia," but it is only a one-syllable word.

Xiang rhymes with "ping-pong." Like the "j" and "q" sounds, the "x" sound is made with the surface rather than with the tip of the tongue. If you say "siong" and make it rhyme with "pong," you will be fairly close.

Xiao sounds like it ought to be written "syau." Like the "j" and "q" sounds, the "x" sound is made with the surface rather than with the tip of the tongue. If you say "syau" and make it rhyme with "meow," you will be close enough to the standard pronunciation to be understood.

Xing uses the "x" sound described above. If you say "sing," you will be close enough to the standard pronunciation to be understood.

Xue involves the "x" sound described above, "ü," and then the odd sound with which Bugs Bunny announces his presence when he says: "Eh, what's up Doc?"

Xun uses the "x" sound described above, "ü," and "n."

Ya sounds rather like the English word "yeah."

Yan sounds like "yen."

Yang beging with a hard "y" sound (as in "yip") and rhymes with "ping-pong."

Yao rhymes with "cow."

Yin begins with an open "e" and sounds like "een."

Yi is just a long "e" sound, like the "i" in Monique.

Yong sounds like the German surname "Jung."

You sounds like the "Yo!" sound students once made to announce their presence when role was taken.

Yu is made with a long "e" followed by the "ü" sound.

Yuan is pronounced with a hard "y" sound, "ü," and "en."

Zeng has an initial consonant like the "dz" of "adz.". It rhymes with "rung."

Zhi sounds like "jr" — it has the same "r" sound mentioned above, and the "j" sound is made far back in the mouth as is the "sh" sound.

Zhong has the same "zh" sound mentioned above. The "ong" is like the "ung" in the German surname "Jung."

Zhou sounds like "Joe," except that the tongue is held far back in the mouth as indicated above.

Zhuan uses the "zh" sound described above and rhymes with "fawn."

Zi has no clear following vowel sound. It is the "dz" of "adz."

Zuan begins with the "dz" of "adz" and rhymes with "swan."

Zuo begins with the "dz" of "adz" and ends with the "wa" of "walk."

BIBLIOGRAPHY

VERSIONS, TRANSLATIONS, AND STUDIES OF THE LAO ZI

Blakney, Raymond Bernard. *The Way of Life: Lao Zi.* New York: Mentor, 1955.

Bo-shu Lao Zi, A & B and several other texts found at the same time. Taipei, Taiwan: Ho-lo Tu-shu Chu-ban-she, 1975. See also Yan Ling-feng, *Bo-shu Lao Zi Shi-tan.*

Carus, Paul. *The Canon of Reason and Virtue: Being Lao-tze's Tao Teh King.* Chicago: The Open Court Publishing Co., 1927.

Chen, Gu-ying, annotator and translator into vernacular Chinese. *Lao Tzu: Text, Notes, and Comments.* Translated and adapted into English by Rhett Y. W. Young and Roger T. Ames. San Francisco: Chinese Materials Center, 1977.

Dun Huang versions. Various Tang dynasty texts preserved in the caves at Dun Huang.

Duyvendak, J. J. L. *Tao Te Ching: The Book of the Way and Its Virtue.* London: John Murray, 1954.

Feng, Gia-fu and Jane English. *Lao Tzu's Tao Te Ching.* New York: Vintage Books, 1972.

He-shang Gong commentary. The commentator's name means "the old gentleman by the river," and nobody knows his true identity. He is reported to have lived during the reign of Emperor Wen of the Han dynasty, i.e., between the years 179 and 156 B.C., but some modern scholars believe that he must have lived during the first or second century A.D. His text of the *Lao Zi* is somewhat different from that of Wang Bi.

Henricks, Robert G. *Lao-Tzu, Te-Tao Ching: A New Translation Based on the Recently Discovered Ma-Wang-Tui Texts.* Contains the Chinese texts, copious notes, an introduction, and discussion. New York: Ballantine Books, 1989.

Kaltenmark, Max. *Lao Tzu and Taoism.* Translated from the French by Roger Greaves. Stanford: Stanford University Press, 1965.

LaFargue, Michael. *The Tao of the Tao Te Ching,* Albany: State University of New York Press, 1992.

Lau, D. C. *Lao Tzu: Tao Te Ching.* Baltimore: Penguin Books, 1963.

Lau, D. C. *Chinese Classics: Lao Zi: Tao Te Ching.* Translations of both the received text of the *Lao Zi* and the silk texts, with the Chinese texts, copious notes, introduction, and discussion. Hong Kong: The Chinese University Press, 1982.

Lin, Paul J. *A Translation of Lao Tzu's Tao Te Ching and Wang Pi's Commentary.* Ann Arbor: Center for Chinese Studies, The University of Michigan, 1977.

Lin, Yutang. *The Wisdom of Laotse.* New York: Modern Library, 1948.

Ma-Wang Dui texts, A & B. See *Bo-shu Lao Zi* and Yan Ling-feng, *Bo-shu Lao Zi Shi-tan.*

Mair, Victor. *Tao Te Ching: The Classic Book of Integrity and the Way: An Entirely New Translation Based on the Recently Discovered Ma-Wang-Tui Manuscripts.* New York: Bantam Books, 1990.

Medhurst, C. Spurgeon. *The Tao-teh-king: Sayings of Lao-tzu.* Wheaton: The Theosophical Publishing House, revised edition 1972.

Pan 潘 version. Version used in Pan Jing-guan's 潘靜觀 *Dao De Jing Miao Men Yue* 道德經妙門約, published in 1800.

Rump, Ariane in collaboration with Wing-tsit Chan. *Commentary on the Lao Zi by Wang Pi,* Monograph number 6 of the Society for Asian and Comparative Philosophy. Honolulu: University of Hawaii Press, 1979.

Silk Texts. See *Bo-shu Lao Zi* and Yan Ling-feng's *Ma-Wang Dui Bo-shu Lao Zi Shi-tan.*

Song Chang-xing 宋常星. *Dao De Jing Jiang Yi* 道德經講義 (Explications of the "Dao De Jing"). The introductions are dated 1703. Taipei: San-min Shu-ju, 1970.

Stone version of the *Lao Zi.* Version cut on stone tablets in 709 A.D. This text was taken as the basic text for Zhu Qing-yuan's *Lao Zi Jiao-shi.*

Waley, Arthur. *The Way and Its Power.* London: George Allen & Unwin, 1934 and many later editions.

Wang Bi 王弼 (226-249). *Lao Zi.* Si-bu Bei-yao series. Taipei: Zhong-hua Shu-ju, 1972. His version of the *Lao Zi* is also available in many printings including Jiang Xi-chang's variorum volume and Yan Ling-feng's *Lao Zi Da-jie.* See also Paul J. Lin, *A Translation of Lao Tzu's Tao Te Ching and Wang Pi's Commentary* and Ariane Rump, *Commentary on the Lao Zi by Wang Pi.*

Wing-Tsit Chan. *The Way of Lao Tzu.* New York: Bobbs-Merrill Co., 1963.

Wu, John. *Lao Tzu: Tao Te Ching.* New York: St. John's University Press, 1961.

Yan, Ling-feng. *Lao Zi Da-jie* 老子達解 (Penetrating explications of the "Lao Zi"). Taipei: Yi-wen Yin-shu-guan, 1971.

Yan, Ling-feng. *Ma-Wang Dui Bo-shu Lao Zi Shi-tan* 馬王堆帛書老子試探. (Explorations of the silk text "Lao Zi" from Ma-Wang Dui). Contains the texts of both silk versions and a received version in triple column format, and also provides much useful information, commentary and critiques of other studies on these recently discovered texts. It incorporates the 1974 mainland China release of the Ma-Wang Dui silk texts, 馬王堆帛書, originally published by Wen-wu Chu-ban-she. Taipei: Ho-lo Publishing Co., 1976.

Yan, Ling-feng, compiler. *A Reconstructed Lao Tzu with English Translation.* Translated by Zhu Bing-yi 朱秉義. Edited by Ho Guang-mo 何光謨. Taipei: Cheng Wen Chu-ban-she, 1976.

Zhuan 纂 text. Song dynasty version of the *Lao Zi* that appears in Chen Jing-yuan's 陳景元 *Dao De Zhen Jing Cang-shi Zuan-wei pian* 道德真經藏室纂微篇 (Compendium of obscure points from the library of the true class of virtue and power).

TRANSLATIONS OF THE GREAT LEARNING AND DOCTRINE OF THE MEAN

Chan, Wing-tsit, editor and translator. *A Source Book In Chinese Philosophy.* (Contains all three texts translated in this book.) Princeton: Princeton University Press, 1963.

Confucian Analects, The Great Learning, and The Doctrine of the Mean: Translated with Critical and Exegetical Notes, Prolegomena, Copious Indexes, and Dictionary of All Characters by James Legge. New York: Dover Publications, 1971.

Four Books. Legge, James, translator. Hong Kong: Hop Kuen Book Co., undated reprint. All but the *Mencius* contained in the above volume.

Gu Hong-ming 辜鴻銘, translator. *The Conduct of Life* (English translation of the *Zhong Yong*). Taipei: Xian-zhi chu-ban-she, 1976.

Hughes, E. R. *The Great Learning & The Mean-In-Action: Newly translated from the Chinese, with an Introductory Essay on the History of Chinese Philosophy.* New York: E. P. Dutton and Company, 1943.

James Legge, translator. *Confucian Analects, The Great Learning, and The Doctrine of the Mean: Translated with Critical and Exegetical Notes, Prolegomena, Copious Indexes, and Dictionary of All Characters…* New York: Dover Publications, 1971

Si Shu Du-ben 四書讀本 ("Four Books" reader). Punctuated text with vernacular Chinese notes and translation by Xu Bo-chao 徐伯超. Taipei: Wan-guo Tu-shu Gong-si, 1962.

Si Shu Du-ben, Xin-ding 新定四書讀本 (Newly revised "Four Books" reader). Punctuated text with vernacular Chinese notes and translations by Li Xian 李鍌, Liu Zheng-hao 劉正浩, Qiu Xie-you 邱燮友, and Xie Bing-ying 謝冰瑩. Taipei: San-min Shu-ju, 1964.

ANTHOLOGIES, HISTORIES, AND OTHER COLLECTIONS

Book of Documents. See *Shu Jing* and Bernard Karlgren.

Book of History. See *Shu Jing* and Bernard Karlgren.

Book of Odes. See *Shi Jing,* Arthur Waley, and Bernard Karlgren.

Book of Changes. See *Yi Jing.*

Chu-ci 楚辭. Collection of poems, some written by Qu Yuan 屈原 (died c. 288 B.C.) and others written in a similar style. The collection is translated by David Hawkes as *Ch'u Tz'u: Songs of the South.* New York: Viking Penguin, 1985.

Fung, Yu-lan. *A History of Chinese Philosophy.* Translated by Derk Bodde. Two volumes. Princeton: Princeton University Press, 1952-1953.

Huai-nan Zi 淮南子. Syncretic work composed under the direction of Liu An 劉安, Prince of Huai-nan, who died in 122 B.C.

Karlgren, Bernard, translator. *Book of Odes: Chinese text, transcription and translation* (of the *Shi Jing*). Stockholm: The Museum of Far Eastern Antiquities, 1950.

Karlgren, Bernard, translator. *Book of Documents.* Stockholm: The Museum of Far Eastern Antiquities, 1950.

Li Ji 禮記 (Book of rites). This is a compendium of Confucian texts that was assembled during the Han dynasty. Collected in the *Shi-san Jing Er Er.*

Shi Jing 詩經 (Book of odes). Zhou dynasty compendium of poetry. Collected in the *Shi-san Jing Er Er.* Translated by Arthur Waley as *The Book of Songs,* and by Bernard Karlgren as *The Book of Odes.*

Shi San Jing Er Er 十三經二爾 (The "Thirteen Classics" and the two parts of the "Er-ya" dictionary). Taipei: Kai-ming Shu-dian, 1955.

Shu Jing 書經 (Book of documents). This is a collection of primary government documents made during the Zhou dynasty. It is claimed to contain some pre-Zhou material. Some texts are regarded as post-Zhou fabrications. Collected in the *Shi-san Jing Er Er.* Translated by Bernard Karlgren as *The Book of Documents.*

Waley, Arthur. *Book of Songs.* (Translation of the *Shi Jing.*) New York: Grove Press, 1960.

Watson, Burton. *Records of the Grand Historian.* (Translation of Si-ma Qian's *Shi Ji.*) New York: Columbia University Press, 1961.

Yi Jing 易經 (Book of changes). This is an ancient divination text that tradition says was written in early Zhou times. With the divination text are several early explanatory texts called the Appendices. Collected in the *Shi-san Jing Er Er.*

DICTIONARIES AND OTHER REFERENCE WORKS

Gao, Shu-fan 高樹藩. *Xing, Yin, Yi Zong-he Da Zi Dian* 形音義綜合大字典 (Etymological dictionary supplying forms, pronunciations, and meanings). Taipei: Zheng-zhong Shu-ju, 1974.

Guang-Ya. 廣雅. Wei dynasty (220-264) dictionary by Zhang Yi 張揖.

Jiang, Xi-chang 蔣錫昌. *Lao Zi Jiao-gu* 老子校詁 (Annotated variorum text of the "Lao Zi"). Reprint of 1937 Shanghai Commercial Press edition. This text compares 84 extant versions of the *Lao Zi.* San-chong shi, Taiwan: Ming-lun chu-ban-she, 1973.

Karlgren, Bernard. *Grammata Serica Recensa,* Stockholm: The Museum of Far Eastern Antiquities, 1964.

Mathews, R. H. *Mathews' Chinese-English Dictionary.* Cambridge: Harvard University Press, 1956.

Shuo Wen Jie Zi 説文解字 (*The telling of simple graphs, and the analysis of complex characters produced from them*). This text is an early etymological dictionary by Xu Shen 許慎 (fl. 100 A.D.)

Zhu, Qing-yuan. *Lao Zi Jiao-shi* 老子校釋 (Variorum edition of the "Lao Zi" with notes). Taipei: Shi-jie Shu-ju, 1961.

Zhong-wen da ci dian 中文大字典, *The Encyclopedic Dictionary of the Chinese Language.* Taipei: China Academy, 1973.

TEXTS, TRANSLATIONS, AND COMMENTARIES BY INDIVIDUAL AUTHORS

Confucius (Kong Qiu 孔丘). *Lun Yu* 論語 (Analects of Confucius). See D. C. Lau.

Han, Fei 韓非 (died 233 B.C.). *Han Fei Zi* 韓非子 (The writings of master Han Fei). Si-bu Bei-yao. Taipei: Zhong-hua Shu-ju, 1960.

Lau, D. C., translator. *Analects of Confucius.* Baltimore: Penguin Books, 1979.

Ma, Chi-ying 馬持盈. *Shi Jing Jin Zhu Jin Yi* 詩經今註今譯 (Modern annotation and translation of the "Book of Odes"). Taipei: Shang-wu Yin-shu-guan, 1971.

Mao, Heng 毛亨 commentary to the *Shi Jing.* This commentary, by Mao Heng and his son, Mao Chang 毛萇, appeared before the middle of the second century B.C.

Mencius. (*Meng Zi* 孟子) Book compiled from the writings of Meng Ke 孟軻 (372?–289? B.C.), the second most important Confucian philosopher. See D.C. Lau.

Moran, Patrick. *Explorations of Chinese Metaphysics.* Doctoral dissertation. Philadelphia: University of Pennsylvania, 1983.

Qu, Wan-li 屈萬里. *"Shi Jing" Shi-yi* 詩經釋義 (The annotated "Book of Odes"). Taipei: Hua-gang Chu-ban-bu, 1974.

Si Shu Ji-zhu 四書集注. (Text of the "Four Books" with collected commentaries, originally prepared by Zhu Xi). Taipei: Xue-hai Chu-ban-she, 1974.

Si-Ma, Qian 司馬遷. *Shi Ji* 史記 (Records of the grand historian of China). See Burton Watson.

Wang, Bi (226-249). *Lao Zi: Wang Bi Zhu* 老子王弼注. Si-bu Bei-yao. Taipei: 1972.

Zhu Xi 朱熹. See *Si Shu Ji-zhu.*

Xu, Shen 許慎, see *Shuo Wen Jie Zi.*

Xun, Qing 荀卿, also called 荀況 (*c.* 298 – *c.* 238 B.C.). *Xun Zi* 荀子. Si-bu Bei-yao. Taipei: Zhong-hua Shu-ju, 1966.

Xun Zi 荀子. See Xun Qing.

Yi Zhou Shu 逸周書. (Lost books of the Zhou.) Believed to be a third century B.C. text.

Zhuang Zi. See Zhuang, Zhou

Zhuang, Zhou 莊周. *Zhuang Zi* 莊子 (The works of master Zhuang, 369? – 286?). I cite the Harvard Yen-ching Institute Sinological Index Series version and give the chapter and then the line number followed by the total number of lines in that chapter. The original was prepared in 1947. I have an undated reprint. Taipei: Hong Dao Wen-hua Shi-ye You-xian Gong-si.

Zuo Zhuan 左傳. A history written by Zuo Qiu Ming 左丘明 during the Zhou dynasty.

INDEX

CROSS
CONNECTIONS

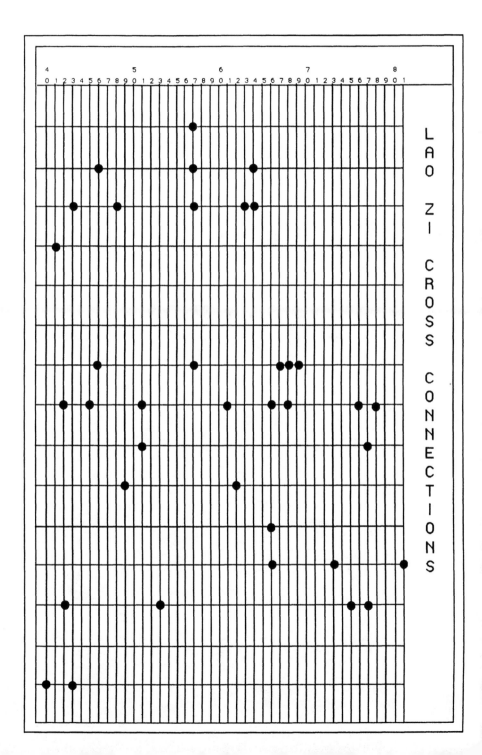

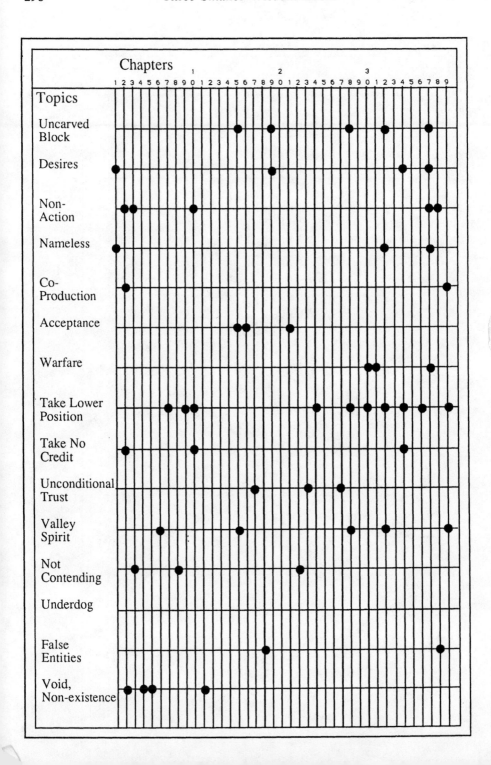